Cope((,)

THANK YOU, JUDAS
HOW TO BEAT BETRAYAL

*Big Faith.
Bright Future.
Jer. 29:11*

TYLRE BUTLER

Thank You, Judas: How to Beat Betrayal

Tylre Butler

Hope City Media
Milwaukee, WI
Library of Congress Control Number: 2015920550
Copyright © 2015 Tylre Butler

ISBN: 978-1-940243-85-6

All rights reserved. No part of this book may be reproduced without written permission from the publisher or copyright holder, except in the case of brief quotations embodied in critical articles and reviews. No part of this book may be transmitted in any form or by any means—electronic, mechanical, photocopy, recording, or other—without prior written permission from the publisher or copyright holder.

Unless otherwise indicated, all Scripture quotations are taken from the Holy Bible, New Living Translation, copyright © 1996, 2004, 2007 by Tyndale House Foundation. Used by permission of Tyndale House Publishers, Inc., Carol Stream, Illinois 60188. All rights reserved.

Scripture taken from the New King James Version®. Copyright © 1982 by Thomas Nelson. Used by permission. All rights reserved.

THE HOLY BIBLE, NEW INTERNATIONAL VERSION®, NIV® Copyright © 1973, 1978, 1984, 2011 by Biblica, Inc.® Used by permission. All rights reserved worldwide.

Scripture taken from the New King James Version®. Copyright © 1982 by Thomas Nelson. Used by permission. All rights reserved.

THE HOLY BIBLE, NEW INTERNATIONAL VERSION®, NIV® Copyright © 1973, 1978, 1984, 2011 by Biblica, Inc.® Used by permission. All rights reserved worldwide.

ACKNOWLEDGMENTS

My Wife Gina—You're beautiful inside and out. You're the peanut butter to my chocolate. You're the love of my life. Thanks for being my everything. I'll spend the rest of my life making you happy. You make me better. I couldn't do what I do without you. So lucky to go on this journey called life next to you.

My Parents—I couldn't ask for a better example. You two have taught me so much. Thank you for all that you've done for me. By watching your example I learned how to be a better person, how to love God, and how to love the church. Mom, thanks for birthing me: I know those twelve hours weren't easy. Dad, I hope I can become half the man you are. You two are my heroes. I am who am I today because of you!

Chantyl & Ashtyn—You're the best sisters in the world! Love you!

Hope City MKE—Can't wait to see what God does through us as we serve our great city of Milwaukee. Our future is bright!

Some Close Friends—You know who you are. Thank you for always pushing me towards my calling. Life is better when you do it with people you love, and with people who make you better. That's you!

Contents

FOREWORD	7
INTRODUCTION:	13
CHAPTER ONE: DEEP AND DIFFERENT	17
CHAPTER TWO: LOST MY MARBLES	25
CHAPTER THREE: HATERS	33
CHAPTER FOUR: GOD LEFT ME HANGING	43
CHAPTER FIVE: BETTER THAN YOU	55
CHAPTER SIX: JUST JEALOUS	65
CHAPTER SEVEN: SILVER AND GOLD	75
CHAPTER EIGHT: RIPE FOR THE TAKING	91
CHAPTER NINE: NAME CALLING	101
CHAPTER TEN: THANK YOU, JUDAS	111
CHAPTER ELEVEN: CATCH AND RELEASE	119

FOREWORD

I wish what was written in these pages was not true. I wish it was all in error and only experienced by a vast minority of people. I even wish I had no real-life experiences to validate it. However, this is simply not the case.

I've walked this road. I've experienced betrayal. And I've learned betrayal is an undeniable part of life. It is exceptionally painful, but anyone willing to inclusively love others on the journey of purpose and destiny risks experiencing it.

Sometimes you expect it, and sometimes it comes out of nowhere, blindsiding you, pulling the rug out from under you, along with the world you live in. In a moment, betrayal can destroy years of trust and intimacy and unleash a whirlwind of pain and anger, and a plethora of other negative emotions. Its disruptive nature can upend the balance of progress and stifle the remaining healthy relationships in your life.

For some people, betrayal can be so devastating that they find it very difficult to love or trust again, and they stop moving forward. The results can be catastrophic. Once open and carefree, some end up hiding behind emotional walls of their own construction. Sadly, the same walls that give them a sense of safety (though false) also isolate them. Insulated, the wounded and lonely sever even loving connections with others. They deny themselves the voices of those who would speak words of life over them (some even deny themselves God's voice). (Loneliness and isolation have been found to kill more people than cigarettes each year.)

Perhaps the most deflating part of betrayal knowing that it is relatively unknown except amongst those with the willingness to love. In other words, it's virtually impossible to be truly betrayed without having loved someone immensely. They have to be in your arms to have the proximity needed to stab you in the back. The truth is, the closer someone is to you, the greater the excruciating pain of the betrayal.

This is the dichotomy of love. When we love, we open up a part of ourselves to be blessed extravagantly, but risk being hurt wholeheartedly.

To bring this full circle, betrayal is a very unfortunate part of every life, and even our Savior Jesus was not exempt. Some of those who shouted, "Hosanna!" upon his triumphal entry into Jerusalem were likely some of the same ones who shouted, "Crucify Him!" at His sentencing. In my heart of hearts, however, I do not perceive these events to be nearly as devastating as having one of His own twelve disciples turn his back on Him.

The Bible lets us in on this relationship. While the Word of God is not exhaustive, we are privy to know that Jesus spent years with Judas. Jesus invested himself and his time into Judas. He walked with him and shared life and ministry experiences with him. Yet in the end, Judas would turn his back, sell Jesus out for thirty pieces of silver, and identify Him to His enemies with a kiss. Although the betrayal was biblically purposeful, I simply cannot imagine the moment when Jesus watched a life in which He had invested His life simply turn and sell itself short of greatness and eternal purpose.

I recently wrote a book entitled, *Buried: Navigating the Transitions of Life*. The book focuses on John 19:38-42, and highlights a tumultuous time not just in the destiny transition for Christ (His death, burial, and resurrection), but in the lives of those coping with what happened to their leader, the Messiah. In the book, I highlight the agony and trauma of life that is still completely necessary for purpose. I call it the After This season.

After This is the initial moment of response to the tragedy and trauma of the betrayals of life. The truth is, if we do not confront these moments with God's help, we will live as hostages to them, and be haunted by them in every new God-given opportunity.

Betrayal was and is never God's plan. His intention is for us to rise from our hurt and pain, and realize that God is not a man and move forward, find healing, and continue to flourish in our purpose. Wouldn't it be a shame to be gifted, anointed, called, and destined, only to be sidelined from all of it because of our unwillingness to confront the root of trauma in our lives.

Trust me, the intention behind betrayal is not nice. Betrayal that lives without being confronted is as dangerous as any major disease. Its root can rob us of the supply that being connected to people in the body of Christ gives. The apostle Paul talked about this principle in Ephesians 4:16 (NKJV), stating, ". . . every joint supplies." Paul is telling us the value of remaining connected and grafted into the body of Christ. This connection helps to release our supply and receive the supply of those with whom we are connected. Without our connections we remain isolated and empty. Betrayal revels in this.

This is why this book will bless you more than you might imagine. Tylre Butler has taken something most people have experienced, yet so few have discussed, and brought answers, hope, and biblical truth to the forefront. By reading this book you will literally set yourself up for success, even in the midst of what might be one of the most terrible moments of your life. If you've been betrayed, are going through a betrayal event, or are anxious to gather information so you can be proactive concerning betrayal, then you've made the right choice by taking the journey of diving into this book.

The lessons in these pages are priceless, and the personal perspective is refreshingly authentic and real. If we can beat betrayal, we can lay hold to the trophy of our call as overcomers. Now, enjoy this journey, grab a pen and thank you card, and prepare to thank your Judas. I think you'll find that the entire time . . . he or she was necessary.

Josh Carter
International Evangelist and Author

SOME THINGS TO KEEP IN MIND

- Judas is not gender specific. When I use "he" or any other masculine pronoun, it is simply because Judas was a man. The principles talked about in this book and the behaviors of betrayal are true of both genders.

- Every one of us has exhibited behaviors of betrayal from time to time. Every one of us has betrayed others or ourselves, on occasion. I present the principles in this book as if the reader is identifying the Judases in his or her life. All principles are applicable if the reader is trying to identify the Judas inside his or her character as well.

- I'm a pastor and a preacher. I believe in the Bible. You can find the story of Jesus and Judas in the Bible. I believe that the Bible is absolute truth. I derive the principles in this book from the Bible. However, I believe that even if you are not a Christian, or don't believe in the Bible, this book can help you. Whether you believe the Bible is true or not, put your bias aside and I promise the principles in this book will apply to your life.

- Not only am I a preacher, but I'm a man. I have a sense of humor. I'm sarcastic. I write the way I talk in real life. I tell jokes. I like to have fun. I believe life is to be enjoyed, not endured. Have some fun with me. Use the pains and pleasures presented in the pages of my story to help you. Let's have fun and go on this journey together.

INTRODUCTION

I'm a twenty-seven-year-old man from Racine, Wisconsin. I enjoy anything that can be turned into a competition, any combination of peanut butter and chocolate, and retro Jordans. My television is permanently fixed on ESPN, and I like to run and do CrossFit—and by "like to" I mean "have to." Otherwise, I gain weight faster than the time it will take you to read this introduction. I am also a pastor for the church I grew up in.

It's that last part I'm most proud of. I have the honor of serving in the same church that helped raise me. From time to time a senior member of our church community reminds me of that fact. There's nothing like preaching your guts out, walking off stage, and hearing: "That was so good Tylre. I remember when I used to change your diapers." It's awkward and awesome at the same time.

I want to clear up a misconception: Just because I'm a pastor doesn't mean I'm perfect. It's only by the grace of God that I have the privilege to do what I get to do on a daily basis. I still make plenty of mistakes, still have "stuff" I have to deal with, and still need Jesus. Want an example? Ok, no problem—I have plenty.

I help coach freshman basketball at our local public high school. I'm not the head coach; I'm the assistant freshman coach. That's like the bottom of the coaching totem pole. And last season, I led all the coaches on all levels in technical fouls. Pretty impressive, huh?

Recently, I was politely uninvited to play in a Friday morning pickup basketball game because I was too physical and aggressive. What? Don't judge me. The Lord isn't finished working on me yet.

What am I trying to convey? It's obvious I'm not perfect. I definitely don't have all the answers, but pastoring has taught me so much. I have seen so many scenarios unfold, been in the middle of so many situations, and been thrown into so many circumstances, and they have stretched my capacity both as a leader and as a man.

One thing I have seen so many pastors go through is the reality of being betrayed. My parents are pastors, and I have seen them betrayed several times through the years. Anytime you are in a leadership position you have a target on your back. You might be a CEO of a company, an owner of your own business, or a manager at your job: with elevation comes expectation. And when you don't meet the expectations placed on you from those below you, they might just try to level the playing field by betraying you.

As you've encountered betrayals you might have had questions like, "How did we not see this coming?" and "Surely there were some signs along the way to alert us to a possible betrayal, right?"

The older I've become and the more experience I've gained, I now realize two things: 1) There are specific betrayal behaviors, and; 2) A betrayal can be a blessing.

In this book we will look at the most infamous betrayal in history—the story of Judas and Jesus. Judas shows us five behaviors of betrayal including:
  Pride
  Jealousy
  Operating With an Inverted Value System
  Selfishness
  Being Fake

We will also explore the idea that betrayals are not always a bad thing. Perhaps what "they" did to you in the past made you who you are today. Could it be that what you had to go through pushed you towards becoming the person God created you to be? Maybe, just maybe, you have been the benefactor of a betrayal—though it could have made you bitter, it made you better.

There is extreme power and freedom in forgiving, releasing, and thanking the people who tried to destroy you. You beat betrayal when you lose the right to hold the grudge. You beat betrayal when you call Judas "friend." You beat betrayal when you understand it might have broken you in the short term, but it blessed you in the long term. You beat betrayal when you thank the betrayer for pushing you towards your destiny.

Thank you, Judas.

I encourage you to go on this journey with me. I hope I make you laugh with my dry, sarcastic sense of humor. I also hope I help you identify the Judases of your past and present. But most of all, I pray that open wounds from past pains will be healed, Judases in your life will be forgiven, and you will be able to move forward with a renewed sense of forgiveness, clarity, and passion for all your future may hold. I truly believe that no matter what you've gone through, the best is yet to come!

CHAPTER ONE
DEEP AND DIFFERENT

"Tylre, guess who is leaving the church?" my mom asked. I was on the phone with both my parents, and unfortunately, at the time they were enduring one of the hardest and most painful seasons I had ever seen them walk through. The conversation was one we'd had more frequently than either of us would have preferred over the course of just a few weeks. One more of a growing number of young couples had decided to leave their church.

My parents are pastors, and have been my whole life. In 1986, they moved from Indianapolis, Indiana, to Racine, Wisconsin without knowing a single person. They made a commitment to give their lives to "building the local church." They gave their blood, sweat, and tears to see the church grow and prosper. That would be cliché if it weren't so true.

This departing young couple was the latest of several to do so. All of these couples had supplied energy, life, and resources to my parent's church. They were all in the same "young marrieds" small group, led by two of my parents' most highly trusted and dearly loved staff members, a husband and wife.

Due to their position and power, this couple had a high level of influence, especially within their small group. Looking back on the situation now, it is easy to see how they began to draw people to themselves and their vision rather than to the vision for the church prayerfully cast by the senior pastors, my parents. I guess hindsight is 20/20, but that doesn't make it any easier to deal with.

This couple was one my parents never would have thought would betray them. They were close, they were loved, and they were treated with respect and honor. As "ministry gigs" go, they had it pretty easy. In spite of all this, they began to spread rumors and lies about my parents and the church. They were unrelenting and strategic in their divisive plan. They wanted to cause as much pain as they could—and they did.

My parents had been betrayed before. When you're a pastor, it comes with the position—it's almost expected. But this betrayal cut deeper and hurt far worse than others. It's hard to explain, but there's no pain quite like that of betrayal by someone you never thought would hurt you.

Not only did it crush my parents, but it devastated me. It's easier to deal with a betrayal firsthand than sit on the sidelines and watch someone you love walk through it. That season was heartbreaking. There was nothing I could do except pick up the phone and listen to the all too familiar question, "Tylre, guess who is leaving the church?"

Betrayals don't just affect the person being betrayed. There is a wake, force field, blast zone—whatever you want to call it—that goes beyond the person being betrayed, and it affects countless others as well. Anyone in close proximity can be overcome by the toxicity of a betrayal. Betrayals often have a single target, but the backlash can hurt anyone and everyone in the way.

The betrayal my parents endured did not just hurt them. It affected my two sisters and I, the rest of the church, friends of my parents, and others as well. Betrayals hurt deep and they hurt differently than any other pain you will ever face.

Have you ever felt betrayed? Stabbed in the back? Have you ever experienced moments in your life when you thought you would never get over what just happened to you? Are you still dressing up wounds from the past? Are you holding on to grudges from people who have hurt you? Even as you are reading this story, perhaps you recall moments in your own life when you experienced feelings like I did.

Here's what people often fail to realize when it comes to betrayal: perception is reality. If a person feels like they've been betrayed, then they have. In THAT moment, the moment when you feel like your world is crashing, it doesn't really matter what the other person's intentions were. All that matters—and all that you can focus on—is how it made you feel. The interesting thing about human nature is that we judge everyone else on their actions, but want to be judged on our intentions. (But that's a different book for a different day.)

There are few pains that cut deeper than betrayal. I've been lied to. I've been talked about. I've been disappointed in people's actions and responses. I've felt guilty for things I did and was not proud of. I've gone through seasons when doubt crept in and the voice in my head said I wasn't good enough. I've battled with weight issues my whole life and have had to deal with the emotional merry-go-round that goes with that. I have had people say things about me, my family, my church, and my ministry that have hurt tremendously. However, in my opinion, nothing cuts deeper or hurts worse than betrayal.

Betrayal can cause a person to question the purpose of his or her very existence. Betrayal can send a person into a season of depression that feels like it will never end. Betrayal can cause a person to question whether or not God even exists. Betrayal can make a person wonder if he or she has truly been called by God, is genuinely anointed, or chosen. A betrayal can leave a person asking, "God, if you really do love me, then why did you make me go through this?"

One of the reasons I believe betrayals hurt so much is that they often come from people who are closest to you. A betrayal from a stranger—someone you've never met before—can hurt, but you can usually recover from it pretty quickly. A betrayal from an acquaintance can be painful, but you can usually forget it soon after. A betrayal from an enemy is almost to be expected. (I mean, there is a reason they are your enemy.) But few pains can cause wounds that go deeper than the betrayal of a friend.

An Unlikely Character

It can be the people closest to us that hurt us the most. I've experienced it. You might have experienced it. Jesus definitely experienced it.

If anyone could have lived a life free of betrayal, it would have been Jesus. Jesus was completely God and yet, in the matchless sovereignty of God, completely man. It's hard to comprehend an all God/all man person living life as we do, but that was Jesus. God put on skin and bones and lived with His creation. That's one of the things I love most about my God: He loves me enough to one day deliver me from earth to heaven, and He also loves me enough to deliver His Son Jesus from heaven to earth.

Jesus was a perfect, sinless man. His life was choreographed by the Creator. His movements were monitored by the Master. Nothing happened in His life by accident or by circumstance. And yet, despite all these facts, Judas still showed up in the narrative of the boy from Nazareth.

Judas was not only in the story; he was one of twelve men chosen to make sure the story continued. Judas was one of the disciples—one of the people on the planet closest to Jesus. This was by design and not by default.

Jesus knew that one day you and I would face betrayal. He knew you'd be reading this book hoping to find answers on how to heal from the kiss of a betrayer. It is mind-blowing to me that Jesus made sure to deal with Judas so you and I would know how to deal with our own betrayers. In His omniscience, God wrote Judas into the script. He wants to let you know—and I want to let you know—that it is possible to beat betrayal. We just have to be more like Jesus. It's as easy as it sounds. It's as hard as it sounds.

> "He loves me enough to one day deliver me from earth to heaven, and He also loves me enough to deliver His Son Jesus from heaven to earth."

I've come to the conclusion that it is impossible to completely stop people from betraying you—it's simply a part of life. I have yet to meet a person (at least a grown adult), who has been completely shielded from the wound of a friend somewhere along the way. Jesus was betrayed, so chances are we will be betrayed—usually numerous times throughout our lives. This might sound horrible, but trust me, I'm not trying to paint a dark picture for you. I'm just saying that if Jesus had to deal with Judas, you will most likely have to deal with him (or her) from time to time.

Judas Is Necessary

It is my hope that we will go on a journey together through the pages of this book. It is my desire that we will look at betrayal through a different lens. Perhaps betrayal is not always a bad thing. It might even be exactly what we need at times. I'm not trying to minimize what you've gone through, or the pain of your past, but I am suggesting that perhaps there is a purpose behind the pain—a greater anointing on the other side of the betrayer's accusation. There could be a bigger calling on the other side of their cheating.

I just want to tell you that God is a pro at taking what the enemy meant for evil and turning it around for our good. God takes great pleasure in bringing hope into hopeless situations, bringing light into dark seasons, and bringing blessings out of betrayal. Maybe, just maybe, Judas was not only necessary for the journey of Jesus, but necessary for my journey and yours as well. You see, the betrayal my parents went through was painful, but it had purpose. It made them lean on God in a new way. Over time, it made the church stronger than it had ever been. And it taught me lessons I couldn't pay for.

I've learned through my healing process that if you can trust God long enough and far enough, He will turn the rocks thrown at you by your betrayers into building blocks for your breakthrough and your blessing.

> **"God takes great pleasure in bringing hope into hopeless situations, bringing light into dark seasons, and bringing blessings out of betrayal."**

It is possible to beat betrayal. It might not be easy or pleasant, but it is possible. It can be a daunting task. It can be a painful process. But I want you to know that even though what you suffered might have been painful, it had purpose. I understand it might have made you question God a time or two. I understand you might have cried yourself to sleep night after night, wishing it were all over. However, I want you to know that even though it hurt, in the grand scheme, it might have been helpful. It might have thrown you into a season of depression, but it did not deter you from your destiny.

Betrayers want to position you in a place where you'll be forever known by what they did to you. I want you to know your past does not dictate your future. Your future is bright. The best is yet to come. They tried to kill you, but they only made you stronger. They could have made you bitter, but they made you better. This is how you beat betrayal.

Dive Into Five Questions

1. When have you been betrayed?
2. How did it make you feel?
3. What were the consequences of the betrayal?
4. How did it affect your life?
5. Have you seen any good come from the betrayal?

CHAPTER TWO
LOST MY MARBLES

I was so angry I wanted to punch him in the face. Got your attention?

I grew up in a typical Midwestern city: Racine, Wisconsin (yes, Wisconsin). No, not everyone in Wisconsin likes cheese or grows up milking cows. No, not everyone is a Packers fan. There, glad we got that settled.

The neighborhood I grew up in was right next to a community park. I couldn't have asked for anything better. A group of about twelve boys my age were all within a Huffy ride away. My best friend was Jory. (Jory has nothing to do with my story, but I wanted to give him a shout-out. What's good, Jory?) Every day after school, we all had the same routine: Get home as fast as you can, change into playclothes, and get out to the yard for another game of tackle football. It was an eight-year-old's dream come true. I remember sitting in school all day thinking about two things: Recess, and getting home to dominate at tackle football. (I have so many memories of grass-stained Arizona jeans. I wore size "Husky." You're welcome.)

Every afternoon, I would hear my mom yell right before the screen door slammed shut: "Be home before dark."

Those were the days. Long afternoons of plays being drawn in the dirt, poor tackling, and prepubescent sweat.

We didn't just play football. My group of friends and I played basketball, baseball, kickball, and basically anything else we could turn into a competition. We also gave in to the trends of the times. From time to time we would deviate from the normal football game to include other popular yet random activities, such as trading Upper Deck sports cards, playing POG, and shooting marbles.

Keepsies

The boys and I got on the marble bandwagon for a solid two months straight. Just in case you never had the privilege to play marbles, let me explain how it works. The first step in marbles is to get a bag for your marbles. Mine was a six-paneled genuine leather bag (each panel a different color), with a drawstring at the top. Then you start to build your collection. This can be done by buying new marbles or by winning marbles. Being the fierce competitor I was (and am), and due to the fact that I was an unemployed eight-year-old, I bet you can guess which method I had to use.

This was how our version of the two-person game worked. First, the players decided if the game was for fun or for "keepsies" (though we never played for fun . . . there was no fun in that). We always played for keepsies. This meant that the winner of the game got to keep the other player's marbles, and the loser had to go home crying to his mom.

Second, competitors would determine how many "cat's-eyes" or small marbles we would put in play. Usually, we wagered 5-10 each. Each player also had a larger, more expensive marble called the "shooter." The object of the game was to flick your shooter marble at the smaller marbles to try and knock them into a hole dug into the ground. When one player knocked all the cat's-eyes marbles into the hole, he was the victor, and to the victor went the spoils. The winner would take all the marbles from the loser, including his prized shooter marble.

I remember the day I bought my first shooter. My dad took me to the local Nelson's Dime Store, and I spent $4.97 of my hard-earned money (or at least hard-saved money). It was a beauty! I rushed home and went out to practice with it right away.

This is where Brandon enters the scene. (Yes, the boy I wanted to punch in the face.)

He wanted to play me in a game, but I declined. I didn't want to risk losing my new prized possession so soon. He agreed to play the game for fun instead of for keepsies. I accepted, as I wanted to try out my new shooter.

I didn't feel the normal pressure, due to the fact that there was no risk involved. I didn't focus as much as I usually would have, and it cost me. I remember Brandon knocking the final cat's-eyes marble into the hole in my front yard, and then proceeding to pick up all my marbles, including my new shooter.

I was confused. I thought we had agreed the game was just for fun. I was angry, but there was nothing I could do as he rode away on his bike. Brandon was a few years older than me, and though not really bigger than me, he was stronger. I remember thinking: *What just happened? I thought we were friends?* How could he do this? I was devastated. It was not so much that I had lost my new shooter, but that for the first time I could remember, I had been betrayed.

Not the First One. Not the Last One.

Each one of us is born with childhood innocence. Until then, I thought everyone in life had good intentions, was honest, and when they said the game wasn't for keepsies, it wasn't. That was the first time in my young life that I experienced betrayal, and it hurt.

The older I become the more I understand how the theme of betrayal is woven throughout the quilt of most of our lives. Betrayal is a dominant theme in Hollywood movies, New York Times best-selling books, and the reason why so many people chat with Dr. Phil about their emotional problems.

It is my observation that most people are in one of three stages in life: 1) They have just gotten over a betrayal; 2) They are currently suffering betrayal, or; 3) They are about to suffer a betrayal. It is also common to be in multiple stages simultaneously!

I wish I knew the why behind betrayal. I suppose there are a number of reasons why people do what they do. Ever since Adam and Eve took a bite out of that Red Delicious, sin entered the world and people have been doing things they're not proud of.

Betrayal is a part of life. It's that simple. It's that difficult. Even though you know betrayal will come, it doesn't make it any easier when it does.

Some of the most painful seasons of life come through a betrayal. Perhaps someone close to you stabs you in the back. One of your friends who once walked with you walks out on you. Someone you trusted cheats you. Or that one person you thought would never leave you deserts you.

It hurts. It hurts real bad. It causes pain in places you didn't even know existed. Betrayal opens a wound that is hard, but not impossible to heal.

Betrayal can cut to the core of who a person really is. I've experienced few pains sharper than those caused by the knife of betrayal. They make you question if there is something wrong with you. You begin to ask yourself questions like these: *What did I do wrong? What could I have done differently?* This is when you must keep reminding yourself that you are not the first to be betrayed, and you will not be the last.

Not Good Enough. Not God Enough.

Betrayal is a theme that precedes even Adam and Eve, and goes all the way back to when Lucifer was an angel in heaven. He was most likely one of the highest ranking and most beautiful angels, but that wasn't good enough for him. In his mind, he was "not God enough." You can always spot a betrayer because, for him, being not God enough quickly turns into not good enough.

Lucifer became prideful and wanted to become like God. Like him, betrayers almost always have a pride issue. When you notice an increase in someone's pride, take a step back because, with pride comes a fall, and it is likely a betrayal is about to go down. When you see a puffed up chest, watch your back.

Lucifer battled to become God, but was kicked out of heaven. When he fell, he took a great number of angels with him. The exact number has been debated, but most scholars agree that he took one third of the angels with him.

> "When you notice an increase in someone's pride, take a step back because, with pride comes a fall, and it is likely a betrayal is about to go down. When you see a puffed up chest, watch your back."

Have you ever noticed that when a betrayer leaves your life, he tries to take as many people with him as possible, and to cause as much damage as possible? Here's what I've learned: Betrayers may leave with many, but they always die alone. Lucifer started in heaven, but ultimately ended up in hell. Betrayers always end lower than where they started, and always left wondering how they started higher than where they ended up.

The Final Say

It's tough when people leave your life; especially people you thought would be with you until the end. Some people may have even told you they would never walk out on you. They said they would be there through thick and thin, for better or worse, through the ups and the downs. Perhaps it was a spouse. Perhaps it was a childhood friend. It could even have been a mentor or a teacher—someone you loved and respected and never thought in a million years would hurt you the way he or she did.

> **"Betrayers always have something to say, but they don't have the final say. That belongs to only God."**

In seasons of betrayal, it's easy to ask God why He would let something like that happen. Not only does God understand your questioning, He understands what you're going through. He went through the same exact thing.

Betrayers will try to beat you up. Backstabbers will try to knock you down and take the joy out of living. They might even try to destroy you. They will form weapons against you. The good news is that they will not prosper. Betrayers always have something to say, but they don't have the final say. That belongs to only God. Even if you've lost your marbles, God will supply a new shooter for you. And if you lose that one, He'll provide another. It's called grace. He's that good. He's that God.

Dive Into Five Questions

1. Can you remember the first time you were betrayed?
2. How old were you?
3. How did it make you feel?
4. How does it feel knowing God has the final say?
5. How can you live with more confidence, knowing God will always provide another "shooter" for you?

CHAPTER THREE
HATERS

I absolutely love the state of Louisiana. I mean, what's not to love? They have given the world so much: jazz music, delicious food, and *Duck Dynasty* for starters. My wife Gina and I ended our honeymoon with three days in New Orleans. A little advice for my fellow Yankees: Try not to pronounce it New Or-leans. I was instructed—more like rebuked—that it's pronounced, Nawlins. (If you think that's hard, try your luck saying "etouffée boudin," or my personal favorite, "Laissez les bons temps rouler," or, "Let the good times roll.")

We fell in love with New Orleans. Bourbon Street gets all the publicity, but Bourbon Street is not why Gina and I enjoyed our time there. (If you have a religious spirit, I am sure you were wondering. You're welcome. Take a breath and enjoy the rest of the chapter.) There's much more to the Crescent City than one dirty street. There is so much rich history—and so much rich food. I thought I had tasted good pecan pie before, but then I went to a little corner restaurant in the French Quarter, and OMG. And then there are the beignets. Don't even get me started on café du monde—little fried doughnuts with powdered sugar on top. Each bite was like a little piece of heaven in my mouth. Is your mouth watering? Mine is. I could write a whole chapter on the food we ate during our three days in New Orleans, but I won't. This is a book about betrayal, not beignets. (Pull it together, Tylre.)

Recently, I visited the great state of Louisiana once again. This time, I traveled to Lafayette, which is about two hours west of New Orleans, right in the center of the state. Lafayette is right in the heart of Cajun country and is pronounced "laugh-e-ette." The accent is a little stronger and the food is just as good. (Last Louisiana language lesson, I promise.)

On this trip I had the honor of preaching for a friend of mine. It was my assignment to speak at three chapel services during a spiritual emphasis week of a K-12 Christian school. So each morning, my audience was about five hundred students, grades 5-12. It was so much fun! (Shout-out to Lafayette Christian Academy!)

The first morning I preached, I opened my sermon like I usually do: I greeted the crowd, honored the pastors, read my text, prayed, and then opened with a series of questions followed by a personal story. Everyone knows a good personal story connects the speaker to the audience and creates instant buy-in, especially when the speaker and audience have no history. (Ah, the beignet story is starting to make more sense.)

One of the questions I posed that morning was, "How many of you have some haters in your life?" Now, remember my audience was all grades 5-12, and some adult staff. I thought the response would be mostly from freshmen who had suffered through people talking bad about their outfit, or sophomores who had to deal with nondrivers making fun of the car they just got. I thought the biggest response would come from juniors and seniors who were dealing with the drama that can accompany that season of life. At the very least, I knew for sure that some teachers would know what I was talking about. After all, they had to deal with kids all day. (And every teacher everywhere says a big loud, "AMEN!") I couldn't have been more wrong in my assumptions.

While a few high school hands shot up when asked about having haters, can you guess where the overwhelming majority of raised hands came from? Yeah, you might have guessed it: the kids in the fifth grade. You would have thought I had asked them, "Who wants $1,000?"

You're probably thinking what I thought that day: *Haters in fifth grade? What could you have possibly done at age eleven to garner haters? What are they hating on, the lunch your mom packed? The fact that you got a Lunchable, Snack Pack pudding, oatmeal cream pie, and a Capri Sun drink?*

Here's what I've learned in my life, and it was proven that morning: The people who are doing the least claim to be hated on the most.

Pleasing People

"Haters," simply defined, are "people who hate on you." They don't necessarily hate you. They just hate the fact that you got that new car, that promotion at work, or that financial miracle. The term "haters" has been ushered onto the scene and implemented into our daily vernacular by my generation. We've done worse things. I'm sure we've done better.

I want to ask you the same question I asked that morning in Louisiana: Do you have some haters in your life? Unlike the fifth graders who went crazy, I'm guessing you actually do. If you do have haters in your life, be encouraged. I know that sounds weird, but haters are an indication that you're actually doing something and going somewhere. People who are doing the least say they have the most haters. And those who are achieving the most actually do have the most haters. So be encouraged. If you weren't doing anything or going anywhere, they wouldn't have anything to hate on and they'd actually have to do something with their life. Tragic.

People are funny. People are fickle. The same people who talk bad about you not having that job, that car, or that house, are some of the same people who will talk bad about you when you do get those things. The point is, you can't live your life for the applause or approval of man. I once heard someone put it like this: "I don't know the key to success, but I know the key to failure is trying to please everybody."

The apostle Paul weighed in on the topic in Galatians 1:10 when he said: *"Obviously, I'm not trying to win the approval of people, but of God. If pleasing people were my goal, I would not be Christ's servant."*

I found out a long time ago that I can't please everyone, nor should I strive to. The same reason some people appreciate me is the same reason others do not. That's life. Get over it. You can't go through life trying to please everyone. If you try to be everyone's best friend, you will end up with no friends. And life is better with friends—much better. If you spend all your time pleasing men you will never accomplish anything. And that's no way to live.

> **"If you try to be everyone's best friend, you will end up with no friends. And life is better with friends—much better."**

Professional Critics

I have spent the last six years of my life as a full-time employee of a church. I am also a PK (pastor's kid). That means, ever since I can remember, I've heard my parents navigate through the interesting waters called ministry.

If you're called to it, ministry can be the most fulfilling part of your life. It can also be the most lonely, heartbreaking place to be. I grew up watching my parents fight the good fight of faith. They prayed, studied, worshipped, raised money, built buildings, and left a denomination all for the sake of helping people realize an authentic relationship with Jesus. Time after time they have had tough conversations, made tough decisions, and left where they were to go where they were called to be, all for the sake of reaching people. They both still serve in ministry and remain committed to reaching people who are far from God. They're my heroes.

My parents don't live for the applause of people. As a pastor, I don't live for the approval of men. I don't need to have people like me. But it sure feels better when they do.

One of the challenges many pastors, entrepreneurs, business owners—and basically anyone leading anything—have to face is professional critics. You know these people. They are the critical, cynical people who seem to see only the negative in everyone and everything. You know that type of person. To them, the glass is not half full or half empty, it is dirty and old. And the glass is just the beginning of their "keen" observations and sharp questions. The example below is typical.

Them: What beverage is in the glass?
You: Mountain Dew.
Them: Is it a diet soda? You know there is aspartame in diet soda, right?
You: Regular.
Them: Well, you do realize that Mountain Dew has Yellow 5 in it and that is bad for you, right. Don't get me started on the sugar . . .

These people are the self-anointed, self-appointed professional critics. They act as if they're getting paid to sit back and critique your life. They are the Roger Ebert of your every move. They are the Rotten Tomatoes who judge your very being. I want to ask them, "Don't you have anything better to do with your time?" They obviously don't. It's sad.

Professional critics are just haters disguised as help. They want to pick apart every single move you make, but want it to come across as sincere. Their motive and their mouth don't match. They want to tell you what's wrong about you, but present it as if they feel bad for you and want to help you. Critics want you to feel like you need their applause for you to feel good about yourself. A critic needs to be needed; otherwise he or she feels useless.

I've seen this type of person operate in my sphere of influence, unfortunately. Every church has them. My parents have had to deal with them. I have had to deal with them.

In the church context, it's always the person who serves the least who says the most. It's the person who comes in late, sits on the back row, and doesn't worship who wants to rate your sermon from 1-10. They are drawn to or responsible for entire websites dedicated to showing the world what's "wrong" with major ministries around the world. They criticize and tear apart all the amazing things churches are doing to advance the kingdom of God while they sit in some basement, with a laptop, accomplishing nothing.

That's the thing about professional critics and haters. They sit back and criticize everything about your life because they haven't done anything in their life worth talking about.

You've heard, *"If you can't beat them, join them."*

Haters live more like, *"If you can't join them, beat them."*

And by trying to beat you they beat themselves. By trying to destroy you they defer their own destiny. I love what one of my heroes, Bishop T.D. Jakes, once said: *"I've never met a hater who was doing better than me."* Hello. That will preach.

Perhaps my favorite quote on the subject came from Leonard Bernstein, the renowned American composer of the music for West Side Story and other musicals, who is also known for his accomplishments as a conductor, author, music lecturer, and pianist. He said *"I've been all over the world and I've never seen a statue of a critic."* Ain't that the truth?

Critics spend all their time tearing down others, but never have built anything for themselves, nor had anything built to honor them. Critics are loud but they're really lonely. Pray for them. They need it.

You Might Be a Hater

Maybe you're not the one being hated on; perhaps you're the one who is hating. Are you uncertain? There are some sure signs you're a hater.

You might be a hater if . . .

- You enjoy seeing other people fail.
- You find your purpose in the pain of others.
- You haven't done anything with your life, so you talk about those who have.
- Hearing their name changes your attitude.
- You compare your blessings to theirs.
- You look for any opportunity to speak badly of them.
- You feel edified by watching others get crucified.
- You feel built up by tearing others down.

Can I be honest? There have been times in my life when I have been a hater. In attempts to do something significant for God, I became critical of people who actually were. Those are moments I'm not proud of.

If you're a hater it's not a good look, but it's not too late. Even today, you can make a decision to change your modus operandi (m.o.) of life. Start by asking for forgiveness of whoever you were hating on. They will most likely forgive you. (If they don't, that's on them.)

Then make a conscious decision to live and operate differently from now on. Build others up; don't tear them down. Celebrate people, even if you feel like they don't deserve the credit. Look for opportunities to speak well of people. Find purpose in their pleasure. Seek every chance to celebrate people. Life is so much more fun and so much more fulfilling when you're celebrating instead of criticizing.

I'd rather be hated than be a hater any day—every day—and that's the truth.

Haters Gonna Hate

If you thought yes when I asked if you have haters in your life, I want to congratulate you. Join the club. Haters are a dime a dozen. (I don't know where that phrase came from, but I like it, it fits, so I'll use it.)

Haters are loud. Haters are usually not doing much with their own lives. Haters can be negative, critical, and cynical. Haters talk about you because they haven't done anything worth talking about.

You probably know who they are in your life, but how should you respond? What should you say to all the professional critics in your life? How do you respond to the people who take joy in seeing you suffer?

Don't say nothing.

I know that's not grammatically correct, but "nothing" packs more punch than "anything." Don't waste your breath on people who are full of hot air. It's not worth it. They won't change and you won't feel better. Let the haters hate. That's what they do best.

Hater or Betrayer?

Having haters doesn't mean you're doing something wrong. On the contrary, it means you're doing everything right. Jesus had haters. Do you want to be more like Jesus? There you go. Jesus had to deal with the Pharisees and religious leaders of His day. He had to deal with people questioning His every move.

Who is this who heals on the Sabbath?
Who is this who eats dinner with tax collectors?

Who is this Galilean man who talks with a Samaritan woman at the well?
Who does He think He is?
  Sound familiar? Jesus had plenty of haters during His stint on earth. But He never let what they were saying affect what He was saying. The narrative of His story was littered with the debris of professional critics. That didn't stop Him from loving, teaching, and giving hope to people. That didn't stop Him from being the good news to humanity.
  Here's what I want you to realize: Haters and betrayers are not necessarily the same thing. You can be a hater but not be a betrayer. The Pharisees were haters, but they were not betrayers. They hated on Jesus right to His face.
  I kind of respect haters. I can at least appreciate someone who doesn't like me and tells me they don't like me. A hater will say it to your face. A betrayer will say what you want to hear to your face and then stab you in the back. Not every hater is a betrayer. I think it's important to distinguish between them.

> **"Don't exhaust all of your energy on your enemies. Pray for them but don't let them consume you."**

  While Judas is necessary for your destiny, haters are just a distraction from your destiny. Don't waste your time on the haters out there. Chances are, Judas is in the same room planning something much worse, much more painful.
  Don't exhaust all of your energy on your enemies. Pray for them but don't let them consume you. Your friend might be the one who requires much more attention. I see you, Judas.

Dive Into Five Questions

1. Do you have any haters in your life?
2. What are some characteristics they share?
3. Have you been around critical or cynical people?
4. How did they make you feel?
5. How can you change the way you respond to haters?

CHAPTER FOUR
GOD LEFT ME HANGING

The game of basketball helped raise me. Before you start judging my parents or try contacting DHS, let me explain.

Growing up as a pastor's kid, I literally was raised at the church. Early in my childhood I developed a drug problem—my parents "drug" me to church on Sunday, "drug" me to church on Wednesday nights, and "drug" me to church Monday through Thursday for office hours. (You were nervous weren't you?)

As my parents spent every day filling their time with the work of church business, I was left to entertain myself. This is a tough position for a four-year-old to be in. I could only play cowboys and Indians for so long before the narrative became too familiar. My Playmobil sets were cool, but not that cool. I never was into coloring, felt boards, or any other stereotypical Sunday School activities—at least not on weekdays. I got my fill of watching *Superbook* and pinning the tail on the Palm Sunday donkey on Sundays.

One day, I discovered a room that would change my life forever. (Dramatic, I know.) It was the gymnasium. I guess I already knew the gym was in the building, but never really considered it an option in my "go to" church activities. That day I picked up a basketball and began to shoot—probably about 3,000 straight air balls. The hoop was ten feet high, after all. Stop hating. We talked about that last chapter.

From that moment on, I spent countless hours practicing dribbling and shooting. I would rehearse making the last second, game-winning shot. Outside of the gym I was a short, chubby kid who looked more like a defensive lineman than a basketball player. But inside the gym I was Michael Jordan. (Sidenote: Kobe Bryant, LeBron James, and anybody else who comes along will never be as good as MJ. Stop comparing people to Air Jordan. You sound foolish. Soapbox dismounted.)

In that gymnasium I would dribble just on the other side of half court and count down the clock: *Ten, nine, eight* . . . Then I would begin to make my move—and by move I mean a clumsy spin move that included a double dribble and a travel. *Three, two, one . . .* I would release the buzzer beater from two feet. *And the crowd goes wild! Tylre Butler has done it again, folks. He's done it again!*

From all those hours spent in the gym, it birthed in me a deep passion for the game of basketball. As I got older I got better. My dad would often take a break from the demands of ministry to join me in the gym. We would play games of PIG, HORSE, and pretty much every other animal. I think we played a game of H-I-P-P-O-P-O-T-A-M-U-S once. We probably misspelled it. As years went by, our games of PIG turned into intense one-on-one battles. I'm talking sweat pouring out and drenching my dad's pleated Dockers slacks. (Sorry, dad.)

Those moments are some of my fondest moments of childhood. Is that weird?

Starting Lineups

With time, my love for the game of basketball grew. I was the only nine-year-old I knew who forced himself to stay up to watch random Big Sky and Mountain West Conference matchups. God forbid I miss that nail-biter between Idaho State and Eastern Washington.

In fifth grade I was selected to a traveling team called "Small-Frys." Cool name, I know. I wasn't wearing size husky anymore, thank God. As a freshman in high school, I made the varsity team. Basketball was always my sport. I still love it, and a part of me still thinks I could have made the NBA if I was a couple inches taller. Naïve? Cocky? Probably. I guess we'll never know.

One of my favorite parts of any basketball game was the announcement of the starting lineups. This is the moment right before the beginning of the game when each team's starting players are announced to the cheering (or jeering) of the crowd.

Picture this. The away team's players are announced by the uninterested, monotone voice of the announcer so fast you would think he's speaking in tongues. Then it comes time for the home team. The house lights go black and the spotlights come on. You hear the background track for the Chicago Bulls in the '90s, when all of a sudden, the once monotone auctioneer/announcer bursts out over the loudspeakers with a slow and methodical, *"And now . . . the starting lineup for your _____ (insert team name here)."* The crowd goes crazy. The cheerleaders do whatever it is they do. Adrenaline gets pumping. And the away team is like, "Dang, I wish we did introductions like this."

If done correctly, starting lineups can give you goose bumps. The hair on your neck will stand up and you will be ready to jump to your feet and cheer for your team. (Why do you have hair on your neck? Shave it!) You will be ready to yell at the referees. Yelling at the refs is my favorite part, in case you were wondering.

One of the more unique elements of starting lineups is when players' names are called and they run out to the rest of their team and coaches and begin a series of handshakes. Each coach receives a normal high five but then the creativity begins. All players seem to have their own handshakes. Some are as common as chest bumps, while others appear as complex as someone trying to recite the book of Deuteronomy using sign language. However, the most awkward moments of the starting lineup process (and in life in general) is when someone leaves another hanging—no one is there to share his or her handshake.

It's usually the benchwarmer who gets left hanging, isn't it? It's the guy who doesn't get to play much, sits on the end of the bench, and gets the water out to players during timeouts. Then he puts himself out there only to be left hanging by the star.

I feel like this is how many of us view relationship with God. We are in the pregame of our lives and we put ourselves out there only to feel we've been left hanging by God. It's awkward, isn't it?

God, did you not see my hand?
Did you see me and ignore me?
Are you too busy for my handshake?
Is what I have planned not good enough?

Have you ever felt like God left you hanging? That you put your hand out there but received nothing in return? You've been doing all the right things and yet you feel like God doesn't see your struggle. You pray, fast, give your tithes, and serve at the church, yet things in your life still aren't going well. You pray so long and so hard that you don't know what else to say, and God still hasn't answered you.

I've gotten to points in my life where I began to ask God where He was. I wondered if He even saw me; if He even cared. To be honest, more than once I thought God had left me hanging.

One of the hardest battles you'll have to face in life is feeling like God has turned His back on you. You feel like God has left you hanging. You feel like you've been betrayed—not by Judas—but by God.

Putting Yourself Out There

I believe that many people stop short of what they're called to do, not because of what others have done to them, but because of what God has not done for them. Putting yourself out there is a vulnerable place to be. It can be scary. What if God doesn't reciprocate my reach? What if He doesn't answer my prayer? What if He doesn't respond the way I'd like?

Do you know what "putting yourself out there" is called? Faith.

When you feel like God has betrayed you, it is hard to continue having faith. After all, why should you trust someone who doesn't show up for you?

In my years in ministry I've seen a similar process take place with many people. They come to church and experience Jesus. They go all out. They are committed. They serve. They are giving. They are all these things . . . at least until something bad happens. One prayer goes unanswered or one bad thing happens and they're gone. The overwhelming number of people I've seen leave the church did not do so because of what people said about them, but because of what they believe God didn't say to them.

If you're not careful, you can view the silence of God as the betrayal of God. Maybe something terrible happened to you and you felt like God wasn't there for you. Perhaps at one time you faced tremendous problems and felt like God didn't care. Maybe you prayed and prayed and God didn't speak to you.

What do you do when your faith has run out?

What do you do when you feel like God has betrayed you?

Why Have You Left Me Hanging?

If you have ever felt like you've been betrayed by God, you are not alone.

Recently, as I read the account of Christ's passion, one verse caught my attention—it actually rocked my world. It's one of those verses I've probably read a thousand times, but as I read it one more time I saw something different. I love when that happens. The Bible is alive, so it happens all the time.

Toward the end of the book of Matthew we begin to see the Passion unfold. Jesus is arrested, beaten, and nailed to a cross. As He hangs on the cross, holding the weight of every sin from every person, He says something that is shocking: *"At noon, darkness fell across the whole land until three o'clock. At about three o'clock, Jesus called out with a loud voice, 'Eli, Eli, lema sabachthani?' which means 'My God, my God, why have you abandoned me?'"* (Matthew 26:45-46).

Did you catch that?

"My God, my God, why have you abandoned me?"

In other words, *"My God, why have you left me hanging?"*

Jesus, the Savior of the universe, the Son of God, fully God and fully man, is hanging on a cross and yells out to God, "Why have you left me hanging?"

This comes out of the mouth of a perfect man. This phrase is uttered by God in flesh. This shows us something amazing. Jesus not only felt like God left Him hanging on a cross—He felt like God left Him hanging in life.

In that moment on the cross, Jesus felt as if He had been betrayed by God. Why would God in flesh feel like He had been betrayed by God? He was showing us that we are not alone in our pain and in our questioning.

God knew what He was doing—He always knows what He's doing. He had to turn His back on Jesus for a short time so He could turn His face towards you and me. Jesus not only died for us, but He also died as us. He took our place. The Father had to allow Jesus to feel as if He had left Him hanging so He could do what He needed to do. By doing this, He assures us that He would never leave us hanging. What a beautiful picture of grace, of love, and of supernatural substitution.

> **"He had to turn His back on Jesus for a short time so He could turn His face toward you and me."**

Three Days Later . . .

I am so thankful for the cross. But I'm also thankful that the story doesn't end at the cross. There is power in the cross, but it wasn't until Jesus was resurrected that He had all power in His hands. Please don't get it twisted. I'm not discrediting the cross. I love the cross. I preach the cross, though I have never been able to comprehend the sacrifice Jesus made on the cross. The cross provided a substitution and salvation for sinners like me. Amazing grace, how sweet the sound.

Three days later . . . (I hear a Hammond B-3 organ tuning up) a borrowed tomb turned into an empty tomb. Death did not destroy Jesus, and the grave could not hold Him.

I'm thankful that Jesus died, but I'm also thankful that He didn't stay dead. Good Friday brought us salvation. Easter Sunday brought us victory.

What am I getting at?

My point is that oftentimes in life we feel like God has left us hanging. We feel like God has betrayed us. We feel like we put ourselves out there and it didn't work out for us. We feel like Jesus did on the cross: *My God, why have you forsaken me?*

> "I'm thankful that Jesus died, but I'm also thankful that He didn't stay dead. Good Friday brought us salvation. Easter Sunday brought us victory."

I want to encourage you. Even if you feel like God has betrayed you, He hasn't. In the tough seasons it's easy to question where God is, or if He even knows what He's doing. But we must remember that God can take even our most jacked up situations and turn them around for our good. He not only loves us . . . He likes us.

Romans 8:28 tells us, *"God causes everything to work together for the good of those who love God." Some things? Good things? Only things we understand? Only things we like or that fit our plan?* No . . . all things . . . everything.

Here's one of the things I love most about God: He takes what the enemy meant for evil and turns it around for our good. Though you might feel God has betrayed you, and that from time to time He's left you hanging, it's just a setup.

Here's what I've learned in life: Every hang-up is just a setup for God to show up. He did it with Jesus, He's done it in my life, and He'll do it in yours.

An aged and mature David put it this way: *"Once I was young, and now I am old. Yet I have never seen the godly abandoned or their children begging for bread"* (Psalm 37:25).

You might feel like God has left you hanging, but He hasn't.

You might feel like God didn't hear your prayers, but He has.

You might feel like God has betrayed you, but He's just preparing something greater for you.

In life, every hang-up is a setup for God to show up. And when God shows up, nothing is impossible. When God shows up, everything is possible.

> **"Every hang-up is just a setup for God to show up."**

Let Faith Kick In

Feeling betrayed by God is a tough place to be. And if you let it, it can throw you off course for a very long time—it has thrown some people off course forever. You have to possess enough maturity and spiritual fortitude to sacrifice your right to know the whys, whens, wheres, and how longs of life.

This is where faith kicks in. You have to be able to trust God even when you can't see God. You have to be able to believe God knows what He's doing even when you can't feel Him. If God is silent, it's not because He's betraying you. It's because He's building something better for you. My friend, Pastor Josh Carter says, "Don't confuse the silence of God with the severance of God."

He hasn't turned His back on you. He hasn't stabbed you in the back. Actually, quite the opposite is true. He turned His back on Jesus so that He could always have your back. He's working everything together for your good. God cannot betray you. It's not in His nature. He loves you and sent His Son to die for you. He sent His Son to hang on a cross and die so He wouldn't ever have to leave you hung out to dry.

Betrayal from people is real and it can cut very deep. Judas might have betrayed you, and we'll get to him, but God will never betray you. He'll never leave you. He'll never forsake you. Don't let a tough season or a hang-up make you question the existence of God.

He's there. He cares. Let your faith kick in. You're going to need it in full force when Judas enters your life.

Betrayal Behavior

We can all agree that we don't want to be betrayed; that we don't want Judas to run amuck in our lives. How do we know when Judas is in our life? After all, Judas was with the other disciples for over three years, and none of them picked up on clues of his coming betrayal.

One of the unique characteristics of Judas is that he is a destroyer operating as a disciple. If you could ask Judas, I bet his favorite holiday would be Halloween because he loves to disguise who he really is for who you want him to be. You recognize his face, but it's just a façade. He gets close, but not close enough that you see his secrets or the things he tries to keep hidden. He earns your trust, but is really a traitor. Judas is a master manipulator. But how do you recognize him?

The navigation of Jesus through the narrative of His betrayal teaches us not only what to say to Judas in the end, but also how to identify him along the way. The story of the betrayal of Jesus gives us great insight about how to see Judas for who he really is. I'm not suggesting that you'll ever be able to fully stop the Judases in your life, but I do think you can see them coming from a mile away. Jesus choose Judas so that we could see him for who he really is.

Let's peel back the façade of Judas. Let's remove the mask. There are behaviors of betrayal. Judas is not that hard to recognize; you just have to know what to look for.

Dive Into Five Questions

1. Have you ever felt like God left you hanging?
2. How did it make you feel?
3. How long did those feelings last?
4. What can you do to remind yourself God is in control?
5. What actions can you take to make sure your faith remains strong through difficult seasons?

CHAPTER FIVE
BETTER THAN YOU

Few places have the ability to teach a person a deluge of life lessons quite like the local YMCA, or the "Y" as it's commonly known. The Y is usually a good representation of the community it is in. I've learned so many valuable life lessons at the local Y. I learned how to sneak into places I wasn't necessarily supposed to be. I learned how to communicate and interact with people who didn't look like me or talk like me. And, perhaps the most important lesson of them all, I learned to keep my head straight and eyes up when walking through the men's locker room. I mean, there should be a warning sign over the entrance, something like, "Old, naked men present. Enter at your own risk." You're welcome for the visual.

I spent hours upon hours at my Y. It was the hub of the basketball community, especially in the summer. You would have to wait thirty minutes for a chance to play in a pickup game. If your team won, you got to play again. If your team lost, you might as well go home because it would be another hour before you saw the court again. I liked it that way. There were winners and losers. None of this "everyone's a winner" stuff that runs rampant in youth sports today. There were clear-cut consequences for your performance on the court. Win and you stay on the court; lose and you get kicked off the court. That's pretty much life in a nutshell isn't it? That is, unless you factor in the grace of God and that He always gives you a second chance. (But I'm not sure they believe in grace at the local YMCA.)

Due to how pickup games worked, winning was top priority. This meant that having a good team was imperative. Making good choices of players for your team was a crucial part of every Y experience. It could be the difference between playing four or five games straight, or losing and going home after barely breaking a sweat. Talk about pressure.

Now, I'm walking proof that you can't judge a book by its cover. But I'm a firm believer that you can judge whether or not someone is a true hooper by a few things: how they're dressed, their shoes, and their jump shot. While the current game is being played on the court, it is very important to scout everyone else in the gym to see if they have what it takes to make your five. Anyone who has ever played in a pickup game at a community gym knows exactly what I'm talking about.

Judas Is "That Guy"

One of my basketball pet peeves are people who think they're better than they really are. If basketball isn't your thing, that's cool—I won't judge you. I'm sure you're great at art, poetry, a different sport, or any number of other things. But there's always that one guy at the gym who thinks he is God's gift to the game. They think they were just a few steps away from making it to the league. (Wait, am I this guy?)

You've encountered this guy before. His neon shoestrings match his neon headband. His shorts and shirt are color coordinated. He wears breakaway pants for no reason. He has a shooting sleeve and wristbands on. He does drills in the corner while everyone else waits their turn. And the number one sign that you met "that guy" is he is the loudest in the gym. While everyone is chilling, this guy is sharing the highlight reel of his high school days. He will say stuff like, "One time I had twenty-three points in ninth grade. Yea, I could have played D-1." Yeah, don't be that guy.

I've learned that it's usually the loudest people in the gym who have the least to say, and I think the same principle can be applied in life. People who think they are better than they really are need attention and affirmation. Not only do they think they are better than they really are, but often they think they are better than everyone else. They not only overvalue themselves, but they undervalue everyone else. The only way to build themselves up is to tear others down.

Judas is that guy. Judas is the guy with no jump shot, but brand new "J's." He's got no moves on the court, but off the court his mouth won't stop moving. Judas is the loudest in the gym. He wants everyone to know he's there. He's seeking affirmation and attention. The first behavior of betrayal that we must consider is pride. The Judases in your life think they are better than you.

Welcome to My Hood

The city I grew up in was very multicultural, and I wouldn't have had it any other way. People from many cultural, racial, economic, and social backgrounds all lived within a ten-mile radius of each other. The interesting thing was, every different group of people seemed to stay in particular neighborhoods. Million dollar homes were literally just a couple blocks away from low-income housing, and the people from each area didn't mix with others. It was like they had an agreement: "Don't come down our street and we won't go down your street."

America has come a long way in the area of breaking down cultural barriers, but she still has a long way to go. My hometown didn't quite have a "wrong side of the tracks" dynamic, but many towns and cities across America still do. My question is, if here on earth some people don't want to mix with people who don't look, act, or talk like them, what are they going to do when they get to heaven? Only God can take what is broken and dysfunctional and make it blessed and functional. Not only functional, but fun. Not only fun, but perfect.

In the city where I was raised, I noticed some people who were better off and lived in the nicer areas looked down upon those who didn't. Some of the people in the million dollar homes acted like the people in the low-income housing didn't exist. Please notice I said "some," not "everyone." I'm not supporting stereotypes or trying to lump everyone into the same group. That being said, I think we would be naïve if we said this attitude doesn't still exist in villages, towns, neighborhoods, cities across the country, and probably the world.

Judas is the well-to-do man in the million dollar home. He is the guy from the right side of the tracks. Judas was from the good neighborhood with the white picket fences and 2.3 kids. Judas has the 7 series BMW with black rims and different tires for winter and summer.

Now, there's nothing wrong with having "stuff" as long as the stuff doesn't have you. There's nothing wrong with being blessed, as long as you don't look down upon those who are not. Money doesn't make you who you are; it magnifies who you are. If you're a jerk without money, chances are you'll be even more of a jerk with money. If you're kind when you're struggling, chances are you'll be even more kind when you're succeeding. You get the point. There's nothing wrong with making money as long as the money isn't the only thing that makes you.

A Judas thinks he's better than you, but why? Judas was the only disciple out of the twelve not from Galilee, which was in the north. Judas was from Judea, in the southern part of the region. The cultural dynamic during that time was that Jews from the South looked down upon Jews from the North. Those from Judea considered people from Galilee to be a lower class of people, uneducated, and unskilled. Judas of Judea is the guy in the huge house that looks down upon those from a different neighborhood. His address is his affirmation. His neighborhood is his identity. He thinks he's better than you. He can't seem to help it. This is the first behavior of betrayal.

> "Money doesn't make you who you are; it magnifies who you are."

"At My Old Church . . ."

Have you ever been around someone who thought he or she was better than you, even though he or she was doing less than you? We've all encountered people who thought they possessed all the answers, even though their lifestyles suggested otherwise. You know: The broke person who wants to give advice on investing; the extremely overweight person who wants to give others workout tips, or; the woman who has been divorced four times who feels the need to give pointers on how to strengthen a marriage. Something doesn't add up.

People who think they're better than you usually have a deeply rooted need to be praised. They need the attention. They need the affirmation. They have a need to be the loudest in the gym.

Jesus was from Nazareth, a name that means, "the guarded one." The eleven disciples were from Galilee, a name that means, "circle." But Judas was from Judea, which means, "he shall be praised." Allow me to take some hermeneutical freedom: Have you ever encountered people from outside your circle who want to come in and get all the praise?

I see this happen all the time in the church context.

Not too long ago a new couple walked up to me after a service and started a conversation. I'm always excited to meet new people. I want to know how they heard about our church, how their experience with us has been so far, and if there's anything I can do to help them. So I was happy to be approached by this couple.

The conversation was going great for about thirty-eight seconds until they uttered that infamous statement that every pastor knows is a giant red flag being waved in your face: "At our old church . . ." For those of you who don't go to church, or don't see why that phrase is such a big deal, let me break it down for you. "At my old church . . ." is code for one or more (usually more than one), of the following: I'm a church hopper. I have commitment issues. I'm only going to attend until you do something I don't agree with. I have unresolved hurt from past religious experiences. Of course there are exceptions. For example, in some cases, people move away and can no longer attend their church. But more often than not, "At my old church . . ." is a giant red flag. In my mind, they might as well have said, "I'm here to cause trouble."

My reservations were accurate with this couple. In the course of a five- minute conversation with them, they mentioned that they were music pastors at their old church. No less than seven times, they expressed how awesome they were at leading worship. They talked about their seminary degrees and experiences. They talked about how the last church they were at didn't appreciate their gifts. And then they proceeded to ask me how they could get involved with our music team. Crazy, I know.

On the inside I was thinking, Oh, *HECK NO. You're not*

getting anywhere close to our team. But I said something like, "Oh, you want to get involved with our church? That's great! We're really in need of someone to help clean the restrooms between services. That would be a great place to start serving."

"I don't think you heard us, pastor," they said. "We said that at our old church, we were the music pastors . . ."

This couple didn't want to serve, they wanted a stage. As you can imagine, it was only a couple of weeks before we never saw them again. They are probably at another church, waxing eloquently, "At my old church . . ."

Judas is more concerned with a position on stage then a posture of servanthood. Being in the circle is not enough. He needs to be in the circle and get all the praise. It doesn't stop at being from a good neighborhood; he needs to look down upon those who aren't.

> **"Judas is more concerned with a position on stage then a posture of servanthood."**

Pastor Jentezen Franklin once said, "The person who is too big to do little things is too little to do big things." That is Judas. Judas is too big to serve behind the scenes. He's more concerned with boosting his highlight reel. He wants all his plays to make *SportsCenter's* Top 10. He doesn't want to be the water boy, the manager, or the role player. Judas would rather not be on the team than on the bench. Judas needs the press conference, the interview with *Mike & Mike in the Morning*, and his picture on the front of *SLAM* magazine. Judas needs the limelight.

I learned a long time ago that if a person is too big to serve, he or she is too small to lead. Great leaders don't always need the limelight; they push others into the limelight. Great leaders don't need to talk about what they've done—what they've accomplished speaks for them. When you come across someone who always needs the spotlight, that should be your stoplight. Don't give attention to people who are audacious enough to only serve for the applause of the audience. One of these days their solo will be finished, and then what?

> "When you come across someone who always needs the spotlight, that should be your stoplight."

Birthed in the Gap

The first betrayal behavior is that Judas thinks he's better than you. A good indicator of people in your life who could potentially hurt you is how they differently they treat you based on what they need from you. Don't hang with people who treat you like you're not as good as them. It doesn't matter where you live, what you drive, or where you work; you are special, you are chosen, and you are made in the image of God.

Judas always needs to shine. The shadows aren't sufficient for him—he needs to be the in the light. Be careful around people who always need the stage, the solo, the spotlight. Be leery of individuals who always seem to talk about themselves, their jobs, their marriages, or their kids.

If you've been betrayed, it was most likely by a person who was selfish. Judas doesn't think about how his actions will affect others; all he cares about is himself. Judas thinks he's better than you and he shows it through both his actions and inaction. He's only present when there's press. He's only available when there is a possibility for attention.

Take an inventory of your life. I'm not saying you have

to remove the people who think they're better than you; I'm simply suggesting your last betrayal or your next betrayal will most likely come from an individual from that category. Judas doesn't want to hurt you—at least not at first. He just thinks he's better than you. Your pain is simply a byproduct of the first behavior of betrayal. It doesn't make it hurt any less, but hopefully it will help stop it from hurting any worse.

Betrayal doesn't start at Gethsemane; it's birthed in the gap between Galilee and Judea. Long before Judas hands out kisses at night, he is practicing stealing the spotlight. The superiority complex of Judas might not seem like a big deal at first, but a prideful heart is the incubator for infidelity.

Dive Into Five Questions

1. Have you ever encountered people who thought they were better than you?
2. How did they make you feel they were better than you?
3. Have you come across people who always need the spotlight?
4. How do you respond to people who look down on you?
5. What can you do to guard yourself from becoming prideful?

CHAPTER SIX
JUST JEALOUS

I don't consider myself a jealous person. Protective? Yes. Jealous? No. I believe in protecting my family, my values, and my faith, but I'm not the jealous type. Jealous people are a breed of their own. They often operate in the present based on wounds from the past. Protective people look to their scars for lessons. Jealous people allow open wounds to create closed minds.

Jealous individuals are exhausting to be around. They can read everything into nothing. *"I saw you looking at her. What, do you think she's pretty? Is she prettier than me? On a scale of zero to me, where would she land? Do you not think I'm good enough anymore?"* Imagine a woman saying these things. The whole time, her boyfriend or husband might think: *What are you talking about? Who am I looking at? I was checking the clock on the wall to see what time it was. I didn't even notice her!"*

The spirit of jealousy can be vicious. It can make a person do things he or she would never do normally. Jealousy has the potential to destroy even the strongest relationships if allowed to operate unchecked.

Oftentimes, jealous people have endured a history of being hurt or betrayed. Therefore, they look at life through the lens of past pain.

While the first behavior of betrayal is pride, the second behavior of betrayal is jealousy. When a person has been betrayed, it's easier for him or her to live life in a way that always looks for the next betrayal. They begin to see things that aren't really there. In order to protect themselves from the next betrayal, they take the initiative to act first—to betray before being betrayed. It's a terrible way to go through life, yet many people live this way.

Lazarus Come Forth

Not only does Judas feel the need to be celebrated, but he gets jealous when anyone else is celebrated. If Judas can't get the spotlight, he doesn't want anyone else to get it. There's a story in the Bible that illustrates this beautifully:

> Six days before the Passover celebration began, Jesus arrived in Bethany, the home of Lazarus—the man he had raised from the dead. A dinner was prepared in Jesus' honor. Martha served, and Lazarus was among those who ate with him. Then Mary took a twelve-ounce jar of expensive perfume made from essence of nard, and she anointed Jesus' feet with it, wiping his feet with her hair. The house was filled with the fragrance.
>
> But Judas Iscariot, the disciple who would soon betray him, said, "That perfume was worth a year's wages. It should have been sold and the money given to the poor." Not that he cared for the poor—he was a thief, and since he was in charge of the disciples' money, he often stole some for himself. (John 12:1-6)

I can't imagine what Mary had to go through. Just a week or so earlier, her brother Lazarus had become very ill. She had sent word to Jesus who was just a couple miles away in the hope that He might come and heal Lazarus. Jesus didn't show up in time—or at least that's what she thought. In the meantime, her brother died. In fact, Lazarus was dead for four days when Jesus showed up. As you can imagine, Mary responded to the timing of Jesus much like you or I would: *"Lord, if only you had been here, my brother would not have died."* (John 11:32).In other words, "Thanks for showing up, but you're too late."

That's how many of us view the timing of God in certain seasons of our lives. We question if He heard our prayer, got the message, or if He's even coming. One of the things I love about serving God is that when Jesus shows up, it's never too late, and nothing is impossible. It's not over until God says it's over. His timing is not our timing. God is never early and never late, but always shows up right on time.

Jesus turns what seemed like an impossible situation into another miracle. Impossibility is an invitation for God, not a limitation to Him. He teaches us to not only trust in His power, but to also trust in His timing. Jesus called out to the grave and Lazarus came walking out. Only Jesus can turn a four-days-dead corpse into a walking miracle. Remember, after four days a dead body begins to decompose. By performing this miracle, in part, Jesus is showing us that He came to put back together all the decomposed things in our lives. He came to resurrect dead things. He came to give life—life more abundantly. He was giving death a preview of a movie He would star in Himself in the near future. Jesus is gangster like that. Lazarus's story wasn't a comeback story; it was a come forth story. Lazarus, come forth!

Pour Not Poor

The story in the beginning of John 12 tells us that Mary poured oil on the feet of Jesus. This oil was commonly used as a part of the embalming process to prepare a dead body for burial. One of the most interesting details of the story is that Lazarus, Mary's brother, had just died about a week earlier, but Mary did not pour her oil on him. She did not use her oil to embalm her dead brother. She was saving the oil for something different. I don't know if she knew what something different would look like, or when it would be, but she knew in her heart that the oil wasn't supposed to be used on Lazarus.

A week later, Mary, Martha, Lazarus, Jesus, and the disciples were partying. Jesus was sitting at the table and Mary came in and poured her oil on Jesus. This act of faith was multilayered. Not only was she thanking Jesus for what He had already done, but because this oil was used for embalming, she was helping prepare Jesus for what He was going to do.

Mary poured her oil on Jesus and wiped His feet with her hair. There was such a sweet atmosphere in the room. The fragrance spoke of great sacrifice, of humility, and of faith. The moment was perfect, that is, until Judas opened his mouth.

While everyone else was admiring the sacrifice of Mary, Judas was calculating the waste of the moment. He couldn't believe that someone would pour out a year's salary on someone's feet. He was thinking, *why would you waste your anointing on someone just to have them walk all over it?* Judas said that the money should have been used to help the poor. Judas never truly believed Jesus was worthy of that type of worship. Maybe a week's salary—a month's salary tops—but a year's salary? Come on Mary, what were you thinking? What was a waste to Judas was worship to Mary. Worship can be sacrificed, but it can never be wasted. Unfortunately, Judas never understood that revelation.

Judas didn't care about the poor; he cared about the pour. Judas was jealous that someone else was getting celebrated. The passage says that the fragrance filled the entire house. Fragrance speaks of praise, for the Bible says that our lives are a sweet fragrance to God. Not only do in your life want the praise, but they can't st someone else gets praised. Judas is jealous of Jesus. das is jealous of you.

> "Judas didn't care about the poor; he cared about the pour."

525,600 Minutes

A year's salary is a lot, no matter how much money you make—it's still a year of your time. I don't know how much you value your time, but I'm sure it's pretty valuable to you. In today's world we are busier than ever. You probably have a career, kids, responsibilities, hobbies, and your favorite Netflix show all jockeying for your time. Your time is valuable. You want to invest it, not just spend it. I guess that's why they say, "Time is money." Time is the one commodity that is given to all people equally. You can't buy back the time you've spent.

Mary didn't pour out a dollar figure on Jesus. She poured out days, weeks, and months. She didn't pour out a year's salary; she poured out the time it took to save a year's salary. Mary poured out in one minute what it took her 525,600 minutes to save. Talk about sacrificial giving. True anointing always costs you something. It cost Mary a year's worth of money, but it was worth it.

What has it cost you? Are you willing to sacrifice the present for the future you're called to? Judas was willing to sacrifice the future at the altar of the instant, but Mary had enough vision for the future to sacrifice her present. Let's be more like Mary.

Judas couldn't fathom that someone would pour a year's salary out on someone else. That waste of money didn't make sense. Judas was (and is) always more concerned with the money box than the alabaster box. Judas thought the oil could be spoiled. He valued the money over the moment.

> "True anointing always costs you something."

Your Judas doesn't understand the sacrifice you've made. Truly, he is jealous that you think someone else is worthy of such sacrifice. In his mind, if anyone is to be anointed, it should be him. Judas doesn't understand the anointing has your name on it. It cannot be poured out on him, because it must be poured out on you. You might be on the backside of a mountain watching some sheep, like young David, but when it's your turn to be anointed, you will be called right into your destiny. Is there not another? The oil is never spilled accidently, but it is always poured accurately.

Judas is jealous of the gifts God has given you; the talent, blessing, favor, and anointing on your life. Judas can't stand it when you're celebrated because he thinks he should be celebrated. In his mind, a year's salary is better off in his money box than on the feet of Jesus. Judas doesn't perceive the oil as being poured; he sees it as being spilled. Don't cry over spilled oil, Judas.

Hole Thing or Whole Thing?

After pride, the second behavior of betrayal is often jealousy. If you take a look at the times you've been betrayed, or betrayed someone, you will probably notice some degree of jealousy in the mix. This is evident all throughout Scripture. Lucifer was jealous of God, Cain was jealous of Abel, Saul was jealous of David, people were jealous of Samson, and Judas was jealous of Jesus.

Perhaps the best example of this pattern in the Bible is seen in the life of Joseph. For those of you who aren't familiar with the story, allow me to fill you in. Joseph was the second youngest of twelve boys fathered by Jacob with four different women. (Sounds like an episode of Maury Povich's show, *Maury*, doesn't it?) Joseph was the first son given birth by Rachel. And from the get-go, Joseph was his father's favorite.

Usually the firstborn is the favorite, even now. In Jacob's time, the firstborn male was a big deal. Not only did he receive a special birthright blessing, but he also had the honor of carrying on the legacy of the family name and values. The second son is cool because then the firstborn is not alone. The boys can be best friends and play together. After the second boy, the next number they probably shot for is five. After all, five boys equal a basketball team. With five, they could have their very own Israelite basketball team. Who knows? Perhaps long before Air Jordans came out, those boys in Genesis were rockin' Air Jacobs. I bet nobody wanted to hoop against "the brothers"—the original fab five. None of that is true, but as you can already tell from reading this book, I like basketball. So do me a favor: Use your imagination. Thanks!

The firstborn is awesome; the second is great; the third, fourth, and fifth are a blessing, but eleventh? Let's be honest, when you're the eleventh son, you're happy if your parents remember your name! A really good day is when they call you by that name and not one of the other ten names. When you are the eleventh son, you can forget about your parents remembering your birthday; you're fortunate if they can even remember your birth season. (*"Wait, you were born in summer, right?"*) When you are the eleventh son, it is a daily struggle to guard your food from your brothers. You suck up to mom for an extra bowl of soup or a few more crackers.

For Joseph to be the favorite was highly unusual. The Bible says that he was the favorite because he had been born when Jacob was getting old in age. Jacob loved Joseph more than his other sons. He showed this by having a colorful coat made for Joseph. In today's culture, that would be like Joseph getting a black leather jacket, or brand new retro Jordans. The brothers of Joseph hated him because of this. They couldn't stand it that he was favored above them.

Joseph began to have dreams about being more favored than his brothers, and he would interpret and share his dreams with them. He told them that in one dream, their bundles of grain all bowed before his. In another dream, their stars all bowed before his star. This was the last straw for the brothers and they wanted to kill him. After deciding that killing Joseph would be a little extreme, they took off his colorful coat and threw him into a pit. They put blood on the coat and then brought it back to Jacob. They said Joseph had been killed by wild animals. Then they went back to the pit and sold Jacob into slavery.

It's one thing to be betrayed by a stranger, but entirely another to be betrayed by one's very own brothers? That had to take years to process and get over. But Joseph remained faithful and consistent. He excelled in every season he found himself in. Wherever he went, he found favor. He eventually found himself in a guy named Potiphar's house. Due to some false accusations, he wound up in prison, but even there he found favor with the guards.

Fast forward his story and you will see Joseph is in prison when Pharaoh had a dream he needed interpreted. Pharaoh's butler remembered a dude in prison who had interpreted a dream for him, so he recommended him to Pharaoh. Joseph proceeded to interpret the dream for Pharaoh, and was rewarded by being made second in command of the whole nation.

Here's what I love about the story: Joseph never changed. He didn't let pains from his past dictate his destiny in the future. The very thing that got Joseph thrown down into a pit was the same thing that got him throned up in the palace. He went from a hole thing to the whole thing. That's how awesome God is.

> "He went from a hole thing to the whole thing. That's how awesome God is."

The jealousy of Joseph's brothers could not stop the calling on his life. Joseph was betrayed on multiple occasions, yet he never let that throw him off course. He remained faithful to what he was called to do, and never stopped operating in his gifting. Joseph gives us a small peek into how to beat betrayal. (We'll get to that later.)

A Spirit of Resentment

Jealousy is an attribute that many betrayers possess. Betrayers want the praise, the glory, and the attention. When they can't receive it, they become jealous of the one who is receiving it. A jealous person is a dangerous person because the spirit of jealousy changes the way he or she perceives what is happening around him or her.

Simply put, Judas was jealous of Jesus. Judas wanted the oil to be poured on him, and when it was poured on Jesus instead, he became outraged. How dare Mary pour her oil on who she wanted to—just ridiculous! Again, jealousy is the second behavior of betrayal. At that house party, though Judas didn't realize it, his heart was already hardening. He could have put a stop to those feelings by appreciating the act of Mary, but he didn't. His jealousy wasn't just. It was just raw, unchecked, and unjust. And that jealousy birthed a spirit of resentment that would lead Judas to places he probably never saw himself going.

If you come across people in your life who are always jealous, take a step back. Remove yourself from that relationship, friendship, or acquaintance. They may seem harmless now, but in the future they could cause some of the biggest headaches of your life. Don't excuse their behavior with, "That's just the way they are," or, "They're just the jealous type." Betrayal is birthed in the gap between Judea and Galilee, but it's conceived by a spirit of jealousy. Judas was just jealous, but that jealousy led to something much worse than disagreements after Lazarus came out of the grave. It led to a betrayal in the garden.

Dive Into Five Questions

1. Have you ever been around a jealous person? How did they make you feel?
2. Do you consider yourself a jealous person? A protective person?
3. Have you ever felt like God was too late? When?
4. When was the last time you gave a sacrificial gift to God?
5. What steps can you take to guard your heart from jealously?

CHAPTER SEVEN
SILVER AND GOLD

I'm proud to say that I haven't given in to the addiction called "reality television." Now, I'm not judging you if you have. If you enjoy staying current on housewives from around the country, crazy medical procedures, famous Hollywood families, and people choosing their spouse based upon a rose they receive, then that's your prerogative. Good for you. I'm sure you will be a beast when the "Reality TV" category is revealed on *Jeopardy.* "I'll take *'Pointless Hollywood Gossip'* for $1,000, Alex."

    I watch my fair share of TV—don't get it twisted. I know that instead, I should read my Bible, pray, fast, or do something super spiritual and powerfully pastoral. But sometimes I like to sit in my special spot on my gray, bonded leather sectional and watch some good old television. My spot is for me alone to inhabit. My wife doesn't dare go near my spot for a couple reasons. First, the cushions are sunken and shaped to fit me, not her. It's like a valley of sports-watching goodness. That spot and I have a good thing going. We understand each other. It gets me and I get it. OK, this is starting to get awkward, isn't it? Come on men –back me up. You know you've got your "spot" on the couch, or your own chair—don't play.

If I'm watching TV, chances are it's on a sports channel. There are a bevy of sporting options to wet my competitive appetite. From NCAA and NFL football to NCAA and NBA basketball. From the Super Bowl to the Masters. From the Ryder Cup to the World Cup, there is always some athletic event to keep me interested. I try to use the excuse, "This only happens once a year," on my lovely wife, but I think she's catching on to me now. Pray for me.

For the record; I don't believe NASCAR is a sport. I know I just offended a bunch of you and you probably will stop reading this book now, but that's a risk I'm willing to take. There are some things in life a person has to stand firm on, and for me, this is one of them.

There is a roundabout in the city where I live. If I ever get a NASCAR itch, I guess I could set up a folding chair on the side of the road, pop open a diet cola, and cheer for my favorite car as it goes around in a circle. I'm kidding. Or am I?

On a similar note, baseball is a sport, but it is a very boring one. Let's be honest. The best thing about baseball is the food in the ballpark. Brats, hotdogs, nachos, pretzels, and deep-fried anything make watching baseball much more tolerable. There, I feel so much better. Thanks for having patience as I shouted from my sports soapbox. You're the real champ!

These Are My Confessions

I have a confession to make. Although I mostly watch sports, from time to time I find myself watching reality TV. (Not what you expected, right? I feel kind of dirty, admitting this.)

In the spirit of full disclosure, the reality shows I enjoy are probably not on the top ten list of most popular reality TV shows. I know it's weird, but I find myself absolutely intrigued with shows like *Flea Market Flip, American Pickers, Storage Wars, and Love It or List It*. It took me a while, but I finally discovered the theme behind my obsession with these types of shows: The businessman in me loves how people can see value in something everyone else thought worthless, then fix it up, and finally sell it to make a profit.

I was watching an episode of *Flea Market Flip* recently in which two old roofing hooks were purchased for next to nothing, a few light bulbs were creatively added, and a beautiful, trendy chandelier was created and sold for a couple hundred dollars. The end result is usually awesome, but the part that I love the most is the process. I think it's so cool when a person can see the potential and value in what looks used and past its prime.

I love it when people can see the gold in the garbage and invest into something that everyone else has rejected. Whether it be an old gas pump sign, a broken-down house, a random piece of furniture, or a cluttered storage unit, I enjoy seeing old things being fixed up and made into something new. That's kind of what God does with us, isn't it? He takes our old, broken pieces and makes something new and beautiful. He sees the best in people when everyone else can only spot the dirty and jagged pieces of humanity. That's what makes Him God, and that's what makes Him good.

Treadmill Talk

I'm a firm believer that every single decision a person makes is based on his or her value system. If you value something you will make time for it. So many people say they don't have enough time or enough energy for different things, but the truth is, we always have time and energy for something we value.

There are countless books, podcasts, and self-help segments on television on the subject of time management. Our culture is inundated with information on how to better organize your day, how to make better use of your time, and how to plan out your calendar more effectively. There are more apps in the iTunes store under the "productivity" category than ever before. A person can waste a lot of time studying time management. (Oh, the irony!)

While I agree that time management is important I believe it is simply a byproduct of a person's value system. If you really want to make better use of your time you should take a look at what you value. You will always find a way to do something that really matters to you. If it matters to you, you'll have time and energy for it. It's that simple. No excuses. We don't need more talk shows and bestsellers on time management or energy preservation; we need to rediscover the power of core values.

I married my gorgeous wife Gina in October 2013. I weighed 212 lbs. on my wedding day. For the next fourteen months I valued food more than I valued fitness. I valued peanut butter and chocolate in any combination (can I get an amen?). I valued ice cream, Taco Bell, Olive Garden, cookie dough, and queso burritos from Qdoba. (Is your mouth watering? Mine too. Lunch break?) And I am an "all or nothing" type of guy. I'm still learning the concept of moderation. So when I began to value my sweet tooth over sweating, you can imagine the results.

In fourteen months I went from 212 lbs. to 278 lbs. If math isn't your forte, let me help you out: that's a 66 lb. increase; I basically gained a fat tithe of 666. Coincidence? I don't think so. I guess everything people say about newlywed weight gain is true. I was just taking the prayer of Jabez literally: "Lord, enlarge my territory." (Not funny? Sorry. #ChristianJokes)

Earlier this year, after eating whatever I wanted for fourteen months, I made a decision to value fitness over fatness, and health food over junk food. It was a tough day in the chronicles of Tylre Butler. I read a little saying that made me laugh and helps me keep things in perspective: *"Sweat is just fat crying."* Feel free to remind yourself of this saying the next time you're in the middle of your workout and want to quit. Those five words can bring joy and determination to you at the same time.

As I'm writing this just a few months later, I'm down nearly 30 lbs. and will continue to work my way back towards my wedding weight. What changed? What's different? I simply changed my values. I went from valuing satisfying a neverending sweet tooth to valuing fitness. It wasn't easy. I don't enjoy saying no to hamburgers and milkshakes; I don't think anyone does. I don't take pleasure in getting up early to run on the treadmill. I hate the treadmill. I call it names. I have to repent sometimes after my conversations with it, but it's what I value, and therefore, I make time for it.

If you don't like your results, don't consult your calendar or your clock; simply check your core values. Maybe it's time you readjusted what's important to you. You'll be amazed at how much "weight" you can lose if you simply live your life in line with what you value. Even Jesus said that if we truly value a relationship with Him, His burden is light.

Drafted and Grafted

I'm sure you already noticed: I love sports. I love everything about sports. There are so many life lessons one can learn in competitive sports. Hard work, dedication, how to be a part of a team, and how to win are just a few principles learned in competitive sports that apply across all aspects of life.

For the record, I believe that only the winners should be awarded a trophy. I don't know where this "everybody gets a trophy for trying" stuff started, but I don't like it. That's not real life. In life there are winners and there are losers.

Where was I? Oh yeah, my love for sports.

Like most of the nation, I love the NFL. The National Football League provides so much joy and excitement for me on Sundays from September to February. During those months, my Sunday routine is pretty solid. I mean, there's nothing better than great church services, a good lunch, and eight to ten hours of NFL viewing pleasure.

After the NFL season is over, like most fans, I don't know what to do with myself. The only thing between the Super Bowl and preseason games in August is the NFL draft. The draft is an event where NFL teams choose players from college to play for them professionally in the coming year(s). The actual draft is not that exciting, but it remains a big deal because fans like me get a glimpse of the future of their favorite teams. (Go Bears!)

To me, the most amazing part of the whole draft process is the evaluation phase. For months and months before the draft, experts like Mel Kuiper Jr. and Todd McShay compare their evaluations of the players on ESPN. Just because a player was good in college does not mean he will be good in the NFL. This means that hours of tape must be watched, metrics must be computed, and evaluations must be calculated. The evaluation process is a lot more complex than the casual fan might realize (and by casual fan I mean me).

The evaluation process ends with the decision-makers placing a value on potential players for their organization. The players ranked higher in the evaluation phase will be drafted first. Those players who are ranked lower will be drafted in later rounds, or not at all.

One of the things I love about God is that regardless of others' evaluation of me, He values me enough to draft me onto His team. He sees the best in me, even when I've shown Him the worst of me. Jesus loves those who seem unlovable, and He values those who don't seem valuable at all. He sees the gold in the garbage; He sees the beauty in the ashes.

Jesus values what others have overlooked and undervalued. And because He values you, He makes time for you. Before He created time, God was present. He literally created time and space for you and me. His evaluation process of us always ends with the same result: I want them on my team. And despite all our sin, He drafts us for His team and grafts us into the family of God.

After pride and jealousy, the third behavior of betrayal is operating with upside-down values. In other words, Judas overvalues what doesn't matter, and undervalues what does. While Jesus values what others have overlooked and undervalued, Judas overvalues what doesn't matter, and undervalues what really does. Judas' core values are jacked up. He makes time for things that are unimportant and rushes those moments that are valuable.

Faulty Foundation

What turns one's value system upside down? Aren't each person's values up to them? Yes, and no. I believe our values should match what the Bible says. In other words, I think we should be loud about what the Bible is loud about. Our lives should be our best representation of the values laid out by Jesus in the Bible.

We start operating with an upside-down value system when we stop making the main thing the main thing and allow the trivial to become our total. I think each of us has an upside down value system from time to time, and look at life through the lens of our preferences and proclivities. That why the Bible says: *"The Lord doesn't see things the way you see them. People judge by outward appearance, but the Lord looks at the heart"* (1 Samuel 16:7).

Straying from your core values from time to time makes you human. Staying away from your core values makes you hazardous, both to others and to yourself.

Judas had a history of valuing the wrong things. He didn't value the fact that he was one of the twelve disciples; he valued the fact that he was the only one from Judea, and thought that made him better than the others. He didn't value serving; he valued the spotlight. Judas didn't value the sacrifice of Mary; he valued the money. He didn't value the alabaster box; he valued the money box. Judas didn't care about the poor; he cared about the pour and considered her use of the oil waste instead of worship. Judas didn't just have a temporary lack of judgement; he had a track record of overvaluing the wrong things and undervaluing the right things. He was so focused on what didn't matter that he ended up betraying the only thing that really mattered.

> "Straying from your core values from time to time makes you human. Staying away from your core values makes you hazardous..."

I've noticed that the people who have betrayed me in my life usually spent most of their time focusing on the petty instead of the important. They focused more on what we disagreed on than what we agreed on. They built up ideas and scenarios in their head to the point where they believed they had no option but to betray, for in their minds they had already been betrayed.

This is why it is so imperative to surround yourself with people who value the same things as you. If you have shared values, there is a common ground upon which both parties can build. You cannot go higher until you go deeper, and the deeper you go, the stronger your foundation will be. Many people desire the perspective of the penthouse, but aren't willing to exert the energy to build the basement. In any relationship, your elevation is a byproduct of your foundation. A relationship cannot grow between individuals who don't have the same value system. You cannot build upon a divided foundation.

Here is a basic definition of "betrayal": "Being something different than what you hoped to be; to be unfaithful to what you said you were." An upside-down value system is a behavior of betrayal, because when two parties with differing value systems engage, it always results in one party feeling like the other has betrayed him or her. In reality, the two were never on the same page to begin with.

Judas was not only prideful and jealous, but he also didn't value what the other disciples or Jesus valued. Judas betrayed Jesus because ultimately, he didn't have the same value system. Be slow to surround yourself with people who have a contrasting value system. As much as they say they love you and that they are there for you, there will come a day when they will choose what they deem important over the history you've built with them. Present preferences often trump past allegiances.

Judas hoped a Messiah would come with military force and political authority, and take down the Roman Empire. Judas looked for a warrior on a chariot. Instead, he got a servant on a donkey. Judas is known in the Bible as Judas Iscariot. The etymology of the word "Iscariot" can be broken down to mean "dagger-men." Many theologians and historians believe Judas belonged to a group of ultra-zealous men who wanted the Messiah to start a war with the Romans, and ultimately, establish a new kingdom through military power. Judas would use his dagger, but it would not be in the side of a Roman, it would be on the cheek of the Rabbi.

Jesus was the Messiah, but he didn't look or act like Judas had hoped. Jesus established a kingdom, but not with military force. Even if the end result is what they desire, if the process does not match what they value, the Judases in your life will betray you and look for someone else who better fits their preconceived notions. Judas is not only prideful and jealous; he's very impatient.

Show Me Your Enemies . . .

One of the ways to tell if someone has a different value system than you, and is a Judas in your life, is if they are often in conversation with people who consider you their enemy. When Judas was tired of waiting for Jesus to overthrow the Romans, he went to the chief priests and began a dialogue that would change the course of history. The chief priests were eager to hear what Judas had to say because they hated Jesus, and had been looking for an excuse to arrest Him and kill Him.

The chief priests couldn't stand Jesus because He was a walking contradiction to their values, or at least that's what they thought. He threatened their religious system and made them feel uncomfortable. He healed on the Sabbath. He questioned their authority. He hung out with sinners. But what the priests didn't understand was Jesus didn't come to abolish the law, He came to fulfill the law. He was just doing it in a new way.

I'm so thankful that Jesus flipped the script and changed the game. He gave tax collectors and prostitutes hope for their future. He opened blind eyes and deaf ears, destroyed diseases, cast out demons, healed the sick, and even raised the dead. With Jesus, even when something seems dead to us, it doesn't mean it will stay dead. It's not over until He says so.

You might be down, but you're not done! The priests couldn't comprehend this. It's easy to criticize what you cannot categorize, and it's easy to undermine what you do not understand. I'm so thankful that Jesus cannot be boxed in by anyone's limited perspective—not mine and definitely not the religious leaders of that day.

Judas went to the chief priests and asked what they would give him to deliver Jesus to them. The enemies in your life are usually not the ones who begin the process of betrayal. It's almost always a Judas. You can spot Judas because he is often absent from your friends and present with your enemies. If you notice him having conversations with people who consider you their enemy, he might be a Judas. We are supposed to pray for our enemies, not party with them, Judas.

After Judas meets with the chief priests, the Bible says, *"From that time he sought opportunity to betray Him"* (Matthew 26:16, NKJV). The principle is this: Even if you are a friend of mine, if you hang around my enemies long enough, you will soon become an enemy. Whoever has your ear will eventually have your heart. I've heard it said, "Show me your friends and I'll show you your future." I have another saying to add to that. "Show me your enemies and I'll show you your Judas." Judas is often found in the presence of people who are plotting your downfall. His motive for being there might be different from theirs, but the outcome is the same.

Thirty Pieces of Silver

I could be wrong but my guess is that Judas did not possess much business acumen. Judas agreed to sell Jesus for thirty pieces of silver. There is a great debate among historians over how much thirty pieces of silver was worth at that time, put in today's dollars, but their conclusions vary widely: anywhere from $300 to $15,000. Let's say it was $15,000. That is a good amount of money, but not for the Savior of the Universe—not for the only perfect person to ever walk the face of planet Earth, for Jesus Christ the Messiah. But here's what we learn about Judas: He will sell you for a small amount of silver even though you've treated him like gold.

No matter how well you've treated that person, it will never be good enough. Jesus spent three years pouring into Judas, teaching him, leading him, and equipping him, but it wasn't enough. Have you ever had someone in your life you treated like gold, but they sold you out for a couple pieces of silver? You did everything you knew to do and it wasn't enough. You had them over for dinner. You talked them through their rough seasons. You treated their kids like they were your own. But at the end of it all, they betray you for something insignificant.

Betraying Jesus is one thing, but only getting thirty pieces of silver is another thing. If I were Jesus (which I'm not, thank God), I would have asked Judas: "Thirty pieces of silver? That's it? I'm God in flesh. You got ripped off, bro." The benefit doesn't seem to match the betrayal . . . or does it? If you're like me, you might be thinking that Judas could have and should have received much more than thirty pieces of silver for betraying Jesus.

It didn't make him many dollars and it doesn't make much sense until you understand that thirty pieces of silver was the going to rate for a slave in those days. Why is that important? The Bible says that you and I were slaves to sin, but Romans 6:6 says, *"we are no longer slaves to sin."* Jesus had to be sold as a slave to take our place. He couldn't have been sold for twenty-nine pieces of silver or thirty-one pieces of silver. He had to be sold as a slave so that humanity would no longer be enslaved to sin. He knew that the wages of sin was death, so He took our place of employment. I'm so thankful that when He clocked in, I clocked out. He was sold as a slave so that my freedom could be purchased. Thirty pieces of silver was the perfect amount—the only amount.

Birds of a Feather . . .

It's interesting to me that Judas was paid by the chief priests. He wasn't paid by some foreign mercenary, or by some outside government. He wasn't even paid by the Romans, but instead, the betrayal of Jesus was paid for by Jewish priests—Jesus's own people.

If there's one thing I can't stand, it's a religious spirit. You know this type of person, the "holier than thou" type—

the person who sees all your faults, but acts like he or she doesn't have any. Religious spirits elevate their rulebook above the Bible. They make it hard to get to Jesus as they build so many walls for others to climb over and hoops for them to jump through. They worship customs, traditions, and religious protocol over what really matters. I guess you could say they have an upside-down value system. This is the description of the Pharisees and the chief priests.

> "He knew that the wages of sin was death, so He took our place of employment. I'm so thankful that when He clocked in, I clocked out."

Here's what I've learned: Religious spirits always pay for the betrayal of the true gospel that substitutes itself for genuine relationship. Another way to spot the Judases in your life is, they are attracted to religious spirits. Not only does Judas think he's better than everyone else, but he is attracted to others who think they're holier than everyone else. You know what they say, "Birds of a feather . . . betray together."

Where Did That Come From?

Have you ever been paid in cash for a side job you did for someone and asked yourself, *I wonder where this money came from?* I know I have from time to time. Perhaps it was a gig you picked up from Craigslist, or something you heard about from a friend of a friend. You got paid and you wondered; *where in the world has this money been?* Maybe you have come across a bill that has had the "track this dollar" website written on it. I don't know about you, but I often wonder where the cash I have in my hand has been.

The thirty pieces of silver given to Judas didn't just appear out of nowhere. They didn't come out of the pockets of the priests. An offering was not taken up, and no Go Fund Me accounts were created. Judas was paid out of the temple tax money. This was money collected by tax collectors inside of the temple in exchange for sacrifices.

Where I live, there is a toll road. To use this popular stretch of interstate you have to pay a toll. The temple tax uses the same concept. If you wanted to make a sacrifice in the temple, you had to pay a toll—a tax.

If you've read the Gospels in the New Testament, you know that the temple tax inside of the temple was one of the things that got Jesus the most upset. In one Bible account, after seeing taxes being collected inside the temple, Jesus went and found a whip and returned to use it to drive the tax collectors out. Yet another example of how gangster Jesus was. He told the people present that His house was a house of prayer, but that they had turned it into a den of thieves.

The Bible is clear about how society viewed tax collectors in those days. Being a tax collector was one of the lowest—if not the lowest—positions a person could find himself in. Tax collectors were hated and despised. In fact, one of the biggest beefs the Pharisees had with Jesus was that He had dinner at a tax collector's house. Crazy, I know.

The reason tax collectors were so despised in that day was because they were Jews who worked for the Roman Empire. They beat up and cheated their own people to help the enemy. That's why it shocked so many people when Jesus asked Matthew, a tax collector, to stop what he was doing and follow Him. By definition, tax collectors were traitors and betrayers.

What am I saying?

While Matthew went from being a tax collector to a disciple, Judas went from being a disciple to a tax collector when he was paid for the betrayal of Jesus out of the temple tax money. Judas further cements his position in history as a betrayer. Judas will only be your friend until there is a better offer on the table (or should I say, under the table?).

Not only is Judas prideful and jealous, but he is also impatient and operates with an upside-down value system. He undervalues and undermines what he doesn't understand. He can't see the gold in you because he's so focused on the silver beyond you. The thirty pieces of silver is silver lining enough for Judas. No matter how good you treat Judas, he will sell you for cheap. He doesn't value what you value. What matters to you doesn't truly matter to him. He may be with you, but he's not really for you.

It's easier to spot the Judases in your life if you know what to look for. The behaviors of a betrayal are painting a vivid picture of individuals in each and every one of our lives. Judas is often having secret conversations with your adversaries. But what is said in the dark will always come to the light. A few pieces of silver is not enough to keep a secret. Judas will sell you for silver even when you've treated him like gold. Judas has no problem being a tax collector and turning the holy places into a business transaction. Judas has a religious spirit and is attracted to religion over relationship. Betrayers are often sneaky, but they're not very wise. The only one Judas is fooling is himself. He might have thirty pieces of silver, but he's relationally bankrupt.

Betrayal is conceived by a spirit of jealousy, birthed in the gap between Judea and Galilee, but it grows in the shadows of conversations among the religious. While healthy things grow in the light, betrayal grows in the secrecy of night. Judas will try to drag you into a dark season. That is why it is important to remember that no matter how bad people try to hurt you, God is still for you. And if God is for you, who can be against you? The Judases in your life don't understand their betrayal is setting you up for the biggest blessing of your life.

Dive Into Five Questions

1. Make a list of things you value and how you make time for them.
2. What are some things you need to start making time for (or give them more time)?
3. What have you overvalued? What have you under valued?
4. What adjustments do you need to make in your life to create more time for things you value?
5. Are there relationships in your life that are toxic because they are with people who do not share your value system? Are you willing to end those relationships?

CHAPTER EIGHT
RIPE FOR THE TAKING

You can probably tell that I enjoy food. I think most Americans do. We've talked about beignets, my favorite junk food, and my newlywed weight gain. It is no surprise to me that the serpent in the Garden of Eden used food to tempt Adam and Eve, and ultimately introduced sin to the world. I don't have a problem with Adam and Eve giving in to their temptation of food; Lord knows I share their pain on the regular. I do have a problem with the type of food they were tempted by, however. I mean seriously guys? An apple? You ruined it for the rest of us for an apple? I could understand giving in to a Chicago deep dish pizza from Lou Malnati's, or some garlic parmesan chicken wings, but an apple? I guess some things are just not meant to be understood.

One of the things my wife and I enjoy doing is hosting parties. We look for any excuse to have a party. Groundhog day? Sure. Your daughter lost a tooth? Cool, let's party. We enjoy filling our home with people we love—to watch movies, play games, and so on. And of course, food is always involved.

(Sidenote: Gina and I are very competitive and will destroy you at any game you would like to play. From Scattergories to Scrabble to Spades, no matter the game, we will act as if our entire eternity is on the line. You're recalling my "everybody gets a trophy" rant right now, aren't you? You're asking yourself, *what is wrong with this guy?* I'm just joking. I'm not that bad. Now, my wife on the other hand . . .)

When we invite people over, they ask the same question that I ask if I'm invited to someone's home: "Can I bring anything?" That's the normal, polite question to ask. Most of the time the response is: "No, don't worry about it. The only thing you need to bring is you." From time to time there is that invitee who does not ask THE question. I'm cool with that, no biggie. But have you ever had that person who doesn't ask what they can bring, ask instead, "What kind of food y'all gonna have?" Um . . . excuse me?

Have you ever been around people who only show up when there's free food? You may not have seen the person in months, but they magically show up for the party. You wonder how they even heard about the get-together. What's even more amazing are the people who not only don't bring something to the party, but have enough nerve to leave the party with food. In my opinion, if you didn't ask, "What can I bring?" you shouldn't ask, "Do you have a doggie bag I can use?" (Can I get an amen from party hosts everywhere?)

Four Types of People

I believe that any person you encounter falls into one of four categories. They are either makers, fakers, breakers, or takers. Let me explain.

The category I hope I am associated with is makers. Makers are people who will help make your dream come true. They will do whatever it takes to make it happen— whatever "it" is. Makers are people who are filled with faith, hope, and love. They are optimistic in nature and see the best in people. They are solution oriented and don't waste much time on why something can't be done. They're not perfect, but they admit their faults and use them to get better. Makers will move a mountain to accomplish their goal, or to help you accomplish your goal. They're called makers because they make moves and they make a way. I truly believe that God designed each and every one of us to be a maker, for we are designed in His image, and He is the "Waymaker."

> "I believe that any person you encounter falls into one of four categories. They are either makers, fakers, breakers, or takers."

You only need about two or three makers in your life to be successful. If you take relational inventory of your life, and you have a couple makers in your circle, it is most likely you will accomplish your goals. This is true because you don't need quantity to have quality with makers. People who said it could be done shout louder from the history books than those who said it was impossible. What were the names of the ten spies with a negative report of Canaan? Most people don't know or care. Most do remember Joshua and Caleb gave the positive report and were instrumental in moving the Israelites into the Promised Land. Makers are remembered. No one remembers those who said it couldn't be accomplished. The names that echo through the generations are of men and women who didn't listen to the reason why it was impossible, but did whatever it took to find a way. These are the makers.

The second group of people are those I call fakers. These are people who display many of the same characteristics as makers, except for the fact that it's all a façade. Fakers are only in your life for personal agendas. They say they're with you, but they're only with you until a better opportunity presents itself. Fakers prey on a person's need for friendship.

They appear to be genuine, but only for self-advancement. They're only with you as long as you have common goals, but as soon as your goals shift, so does their allegiance. They're only with you and for you for a season.

Fakers are expert con artists. They often leave you wondering how you didn't see them for who they really were. Sharing your dream and goals with fakers can be costly because they might steal your dream or goal and claim it as their own.

The third category of people I've noticed in life are breakers. These are people who break whatever they touch. It could be a marriage, a business deal, an idea, or just a conversation—whatever it is, they will find a way to break it. The motive of the breaker doesn't matter because the results are always the same. Intentionally or not, a breaker always leaves a path of destruction behind him or her. Be careful around breakers. Definitely don't share your dreams and goals with this type of person, for they will surely break them. Breakers always seem to be followed by a spirit of confusion. They can go into the most peaceful environment, but within twenty minutes, destroy what it took you twenty years to build. The sad thing is, a lot of times, what happens is not their intent.

Identify and try to eliminate breakers from your life. You don't have time to rebuild what they will continually tear down.

The fourth and final group of people I've identified in life are takers. These people always take more than they give, subtract more than they add, and view every situation through the lens of what they can get out of it. Takers don't bring anything to your party, but walk out the door with a doggie bag. Takers view every relationship as one-sided—they only care about how the relationship benefits them. Takers usually live their lives with a victim mentality. They think everyone is out to get them, and this mentality drives them to take as much as they can, as often as they can.

Not only do takers have a victim mentality, but they also have a spirit of entitlement. They think everything should be handed to them, and when it's not, they take it anyway. Takers always show up when there is free food, but won't help you cook. They love handouts, but hate hard work. They are present for the giveaways, but have never given away anything in their lives. Takers suck the life out of every opportunity, every occasion, and every obligation. Takers take; it's what they do.

What's the Recipe?

I bet you know people who fit into each one of these four categories. If you really want to have some fun, begin to place your friends in these categories. On second thought, don't do that unless you're ready for what can be a harsh reality. Probably a better exercise is to take an honest look at your own life. What category would you fall into? What are the actions and expressions of your life saying about you? Are you a maker, faker, breaker, or taker? Whatever group you have aligned yourself with, it's not too late to change into the person you were created and called to be. It is too late for Judas, however.

If I had to put Judas into one of these categories it would be takers. The rhythms of his life are consistent with that of a taker. He grew up thinking he was better than others because of his geographical location, and thought everyone else was created to serve him and make his life easier. He sounds like the takers in your life, doesn't he?

While he thought he was better than others, he also possessed a victim mentality. Takers are often dressed in dichotomy, and operate in oxymoron. Judas felt sorry for himself and allowed self-pity to lower his self-worth. He was selfish, yet didn't think much of himself. We know this because of the amount of money he accepted from the religious leaders.

The perspective of Judas was always paralyzed because he was always focused on what he could gather instead of what he could give. Judas took unity from the disciples because he thought he was better than them. He took the joy out of Mary's worship, and he took the money from the religious leaders. Judas was a taker.

After pride, jealously, and an upside-down value system, the fourth behavior of betrayal is selfishness. If you are looking for the Judases in your life, look for the takers. Look for the one-sided relationships. If you are the one who always has to call them, e-mail them, and reach out first, then they could be Judases. Judas doesn't really care about you; he just cares about what he can take from you. I've learned that any relationship without reciprocity is a recipe for disaster. A kiss on the cheek is the culmination of Judas's pattern of taking; it's the last sign, not the first sign.

The Last Supper

There's nothing more enjoyable than a good meal with your closest friends. There's something supernatural about feeding your stomach and your soul simultaneously. Gathering around a dinner table was a special event in Judas's day. Breaking bread with friends and family was more than a meal, it was an experience. In those days there weren't any TV's, iPhones, or anything else to distract you. You couldn't check your Facebook, Twitter, Instagram, Snapchat, Periscope, e-mails, text messages, or anything else. You had to actually sit and enjoy each other's company. And the highlight of the experience was the great conversation. Sounds a lot like today, right? Not so much.

Jesus and the disciples spent a lot of time together. Jesus spent over three years pouring into those twelve men. Of course this meant they had hundreds—if not thousands—of meals together. But there is one meal that had much more significance than the others, and it has perhaps become the most famous meal in history: the Last Supper.

Jesus knew the end was coming, so He called His twelve closest friends together for one last meal. It is interesting that Judas was absent for the upcoming prayer meeting, but present as always for free food. Judas can both sit at your table and plan your betrayal at the same time. He has no problem chewing your bread and calculating your betrayal synchronously.

The twelve disciples and Jesus were sitting around an old wooden table, enjoying each other's company. Jesus began to tell the disciples how one of them was going to betray Him. They were all shocked, except for Judas, and began to inquire about the identity of the betrayer: *"Jesus said 'It is the one to whom I give the bread I dip in the bowl.' And when he had dipped it, he gave it to Judas, son of Simon Iscariot"* (John 13:26).

What's intriguing to note is that Jesus dipped the bread and then gave it to Judas. Judas was not only in the room, but he was close enough for Jesus to hand the bread to him. Betrayers try to get as close as possible. The closer they get, the more they can take. Judas can often be one of the closest people to you; his proximity to you births his toxicity in you.

Simply put, Judas will take your bread and then leave you. Bread symbolizes provision, nourishment, and benefit. Judas takes what he can from you and then he disappears. Even in today's vernacular, bread stands for money, or income. Be careful around people who only want the benefit of your bread, but don't want to share in the energy required to earn the bread. Betrayers want the benefits but none of the responsibility.

The passage in John goes on to explain that after Judas took the bread, Satan entered him. At the risk of sounding too spiritual, you need to know that consistently being a taker gives the devil an opportunity to enter your life, and can cause outcomes you never thought imaginable. This was indeed the Last Supper, but it was only the last meal for one man. This was not the Last Supper for Jesus or the eleven other disciples, but this would be the last meal for Judas.

Give and Take

I think my favorite holiday is Christmas. I love everything about the Christmas season. I enjoy watching a fresh coat of snow cover the landscapes that surround me, watching *Elf and Home Alone* with friends and family, drinking peppermint mochas from Starbucks, driving by houses decorated with lights and inflatable Santas, and of course, listening to a heavy blend of Mariah Carey, Justin Bieber, and old classic Christmas songs. Everyone is in a better mood around Christmas. Even the grumpiest of Grinch's turn generous during the Christmas season (well, at least most of them).

Now, I'm not a traditional type of person, but I love the traditions that surround Christmas. Does your family have any holiday traditions? If not it's okay. Feel free to use mine as a blueprint for happiness (or not). It's up to you; it's your Christmas, after all.

Our family has built a strong thread of tradition during the holidays, and especially on Christmas morning. We don't do the whole wake up and sprint downstairs and tear open all the presents as fast as you can in a spirit of anarchy. If that's what your Christmas morning looks like, I'm not hating. In fact, as a child, I wished we could have done that, but my mom wouldn't have any of that. When we woke up on Christmas morning, the first thing we did was shower and put on a nice outfit. Now, I'm not saying suit and tie nice, but maybe dark jeans and button-up shirt nice. Then, when everyone was ready, we would head downstairs to the smell of mom's traditional Christmas breakfast. I'm talking breakfast casserole, baked cinnamon apples, and sour cream coffee cake. (I know, right? Here I go with food again.) I can't wait till Christmas morning this year.

After eating until we were completely full, we would head over to the Christmas tree and choose our favorite spot on the furniture. My youngest sister, Ashtyn, usually played the role of Santa, handing out presents to each person. The way we did presents is, we opened them one by one, each present receiving the full, undivided attention of everyone in the room. This process took a couple of hours when you add in bathroom breaks and sneaking into the kitchen for another piece of cake. That process might sound miserable to you, but that's how we did it, and I loved it.

> "It's nearly impossible to receive what you need when you're used to taking what you want."

As I've grown older, I've come to understand why my parents chose to do Christmas morning like that. The older you get, the more Christmas is about giving than about receiving. When you're a child, all you care about is what you can receive. But as you grow into adulthood it becomes more about the joy of giving. I'm twenty-seven years old now and my favorite part of Christmas is watching the expression on the faces of my loved ones as they open the presents I purchased for them. Christmas is not about what you get, it's about what you give. That's what makes the season so special. After all, Christmas, in its purest form, is the celebration of the greatest gift ever given—a baby named Jesus, wrapped in cloths and lying in a manger. Gifts are special because they're given. They can't be earned and are not awarded based on talent. They're given out of love. Gifts cannot be taken, they can only be received. If you have to take it, it's not a gift, and it's not Christmas.

You cannot give anything to someone who only knows how to take things. Judas could not receive the free gift of salvation or any of the other gifts Jesus wanted to give him. He wasn't around to see Jesus on the cross, and he didn't make it to receive the gift of the Holy Spirit given in the book of Acts. It's nearly impossible to receive what you need when you're used to taking what you want. Takers often possess what they desire, but hardly ever have what is required to become what they're called to be.

Judas has built a case against himself. He is prideful and jealous, and lives by jacked up values, but he is also a taker. Any one of those characteristics by themselves could be labeled coincidence, or happenstance, but when you add them all together they become more than just behaviors—they become behaviors of betrayal.

The crazy thing is Judas takes what he wants, and in so doing, ultimately gives you what you need. It doesn't make sense, but Judas's breakdown often ushers in your breakthrough. The betrayal was coming—it was on the horizon—but so was a deeper depth of destiny for Jesus.

Dive Into Five Questions

1. Into which category would you currently put yourself: Maker? Faker? Breaker? Taker?
2. Think of your closest friends. What category would they fit in?
3. Have you ever experienced the selfishness of a taker?
4. What steps can you take to constantly be a maker?
5. What people in your life have shown behaviors of betrayal?

CHAPTER NINE
NAME CALLING

I'm a proud graduate of Oral Roberts University (ORU) in Tulsa, Oklahoma. I know you're mentally clapping for me right now, and I'd like to take this opportunity to say thank you. Also know that by purchasing this book you're helping me pay my student loans, which I will be repaying for the next twenty-five years or so. Pray for me.

The university was founded by the great Oral Roberts in 1963, and through the years has remained a top-notch institution of higher learning and spiritual growth. I'm so grateful for my time at ORU, and I would highly recommend it to anyone looking for a great place to grow their mind, body, and spirit simultaneously.

ORU didn't have sororities or fraternities, but I found the closest thing to a frat that was available; a dorm wing named Youngblood—YB for short. The housing on campus was set up so that each student was placed in a dorm, on a floor, and on a wing. Each wing had about thirty individuals of the same sex. For example, I was in dorm EMR, on the fifth floor, on the North wing, which was called Youngblood. Your wing became your fraternity, or at least that's how it worked on YB. You played sports with your wing, you went to the cafeteria with your wing, you sat with your wing in chapel, and you helped each other get dates and good grades. I won't go into any further details in case you are a former teacher or administrator, but just some friendly advice: You might want to switch up the tests from time to time. (Smiley face.)

One of my fondest memories of college was going on spring break with some of the boys from YB. When you're in college, spring break is something you look forward to. Not only does it mean no school, but it also means you usually get to do something fun. Spring break is a blank slate; it's up to you to make the most of it. You can either go back home to see friends and family for a week, or maybe, if you have enough money saved, go on some kind of trip. The couple of spring break trips we went on were amazing.

One of the elements of those trips that gets overlooked is what I call, "prep week." Prep week was the week or two before the spring break trip when all the guys would get everything ready for the trip. This would include, but was not limited to: trying to lose that last five pounds, getting the biceps and triceps in spring break form, going tanning, purchasing a new outfit or five, getting a fresh haircut, and coming up with our spring break personas.

Yes, you read that correctly. One night leading up to our trip was dedicated to coming up with and learning each other's spring break persona.

Let me break it down for you. A spring break trip with your boys presented an awesome opportunity—you could become whoever you wanted to be. So, even if you were terrible at life, had no job, and were failing every class—on spring break you could be a successful entrepreneur on the dean's list, about to graduate early, with honors.

We even went so far as to come up with new names for ourselves. So, on spring break we couldn't call each other by our real names; we had to use the names birthed in prep week. This was no joking matter; it was serious. So serious that even to this day, we call a couple of guys by their spring break names.

Can I be honest? I just want to come out and say what you are probably thinking: Yes, we did this to impress the girls. There, I feel better. Most of the time it didn't work, but hey, we tried.

I remember on one of our trips, I had a girl convinced I was a first team all-American fullback for the University of Oklahoma who was about to get drafted in the NFL draft. In hindsight, I'm glad she didn't google the name I gave her, or ask me about formations or offensive plays, because that would have been very awkward. She wasn't impressed and didn't give me the time of day anyway, so I guess it really wouldn't have mattered.

On spring break we would become different personas, but isn't that what so many people do on a daily basis? We did it to have fun for a week, but many people live in a constant false version of themselves. They live their lives behind the masks of who they're expected to be or who they think others want them to be. They hide behind whatever façade will help them the most, given their present situation. I've been guilty of this, and maybe you have too.

#NoFilter

My wife and I love social media and use it to the best of our ability. Communication and information is shared faster than ever through social media platforms like Twitter, Snapchat, Periscope, and Facebook (you know, all the things I said distract us at dinnertime). Out of all the social media platforms available, my wife loves Instagram the most.

If you're not familiar with Instagram, it is basically a steady flow of pictures. You choose whose pictures you would like to see on a regular basis, and when you log in to Instagram you see any pictures posted by the individuals you chose to follow. When you see the picture you can like the picture and/or comment on it. It's pretty simply and very addictive.

One of the interesting things about Instagram is that it gives you the choice to manipulate your photo before you post it for everyone to see. It's like an instant Photoshop option. The different manipulations are called filters. The crazy thing is, if a photo is manipulated enough it ends up not even looking like the original photo. When people want the world to know they didn't use any filters, they add the hashtag #NoFilter to the description of their photo. It's an abbreviation for saying: "Hey, this is the original photo. I didn't change it in any way."

We live in a society where people use filters on every aspect of their lives, not just on Instagram. It's easy for an individual to portray what they want other people to think about them. In today's culture, it's easier than ever to fall into the trap of filtering the snapshots of your life so when the rest of the world sees it, it looks nothing like the original. We filter so much of our lives that the pictures we portray are often not even close to the true pictures. It's not real. It's fake.

Judas is the guy with the made-up name on spring break. He is the individual who lives his life behind many different masks. He is the picture that has been filtered and changed so much that it doesn't even look real anymore. Not only does Judas show you behaviors of betrayal like pride, jealousy, having upside-down values, and selfishness, but the last and perhaps biggest behavior of betrayal is that Judas is fake. He's not who he says he is. His real intentions are hidden behind the comfort and safety of his current façade.

If you want to identify the Judases in your life, look for the fake people, people who filter their every movement. These are inauthentic individuals, people who don't keep it real. The other eleven disciples weren't perfect. They all had pasts. But they were all authentic; good, bad, or ugly. Matthew shows us that he was a tax collector and had a scandalous past. Peter shows us that he's crazy and could cuss you out, deny Jesus, and chop off your ear in a split second. Thomas shows us that at times he had his doubts. All the disciples had issues, but the issues never changed their identity. Judas, on the other hand, had presented a picture of himself that wasn't real. And after the Last Supper, it was just a matter of time before he exposed himself. (Will the real Judas please stand up?)

Blood Bought

Jesus knew that betrayal was coming and decided to do what He had done so many times before—He got away and prayed. He took Peter, James, and John, and went to the Garden of Gethsemane on the Mount of Olives. This is a great reminder for us. If Jesus, the sinless, perfect man had to pray, then we should also be people of prayer. If anyone could have gotten away with not praying it would have been Jesus. But instead of relying on His own strength, He chose to pray.

Never underestimate the power of a prayer. One prayer can change your circumstances. Prayer doesn't really change God, for He is the same yesterday, today, and forever, but prayer changes us. It changes our perspective, shifts our focus, and brings clarity to us. I think we've overcomplicated it at times. Prayer is simply communicating with God. It's not about using the right words, sounding really spiritual, or seeing how long you can pray. Some of my boldest prayers have been my shortest prayers. At times you might have to "sweat it out," but private prayer always produces public power.

Filled with anguish, Jesus prayed, *"Father, if you are willing, please take this cup of suffering away from me. Yet I want your will to be done, not mine"* (Luke 22:42). Jesus was in so much spiritual agony that it produced a physical manifestation. He began to sweat drops of blood from His pores. With each drop of blood that fell from the forehead of divinity, He was buying back the future of humanity. What do I mean?

In the Garden of Eden, Adam and Eve disobeyed the commandment given to them by God, and they ate the fruit from the tree of the knowledge of good and evil. By doing this, they were saying, "Not your will God, but mine be done." What the first Adam betrayed in the first garden the second Adam, Jesus, bought back in the second garden. Every time Jesus shed His blood, He bought back what had been lost when sin entered the world. The prayer in the garden was more than preparation for the cross; it was an act by which He was purchasing what was once lost. His blood bought back what had been betrayed. Each drop of perspiration watered the seeds that had been planted from the Garden of Eden to the Garden of Gethsemane.

> "...private prayer always produces public power."

Kiss of Betrayal

One of the most difficult parts of betrayal is when you finally see the betrayer for who he or she really is. Jesus had the luxury of knowing who His betrayer was because He was God and knew all things. But you and I don't have that luxury. Many times, we are caught off guard when we discover the Judas in our life because we never thought it could be that person. Why is that the case? Because not only is Judas prideful, jealous, selfish, and have inverted values, but he is also fake. Betrayers are never who you thought they were. I guess that's what makes them Judas.

The thing about being fake is, it can only stay hidden so long before it is exposed. Jesus was praying in the garden when Judas arrived to finally show the world who he really was. Could it be that the expiration date of most facades is linked to our commitment to prayer? I've learned that if I expose who I am to God through prayer, most betrayers in my life will be exposed. I know it sounds like a simple question but, have you prayed about it?

While Jesus was sweating blood, Judas was smelling blood. Betrayers are predators who wait for the right time and then attack. They pride themselves on being the carnivores of your calling. Have you ever noticed that most betrayals happen at the worst time for you? That's because betrayers are experts at kicking you when you're down. Judas showed up while Jesus was going through one of the most agonizing moments of His journey. While Jesus was praying, Judas was preying. Betrayers try to take advantage of what looks like weakness. They come in for the kill when you're already down on your knees.

Jesus concluded His prayer and was at peace with His destiny. He looked across the garden to see a familiar face approaching Him. It was Judas with a crowd of people. Judas used to be part of the twelve, but then he positioned himself as just one of the crowd. Betrayers are never true leaders; they are always just part of the crowd.

The crowd gathered in to see what Judas would do. He walked up to Jesus and said "Greetings, Rabbi." Judas acknowledged Jesus as teacher, but not as Lord. Betrayers have a hard time honoring who you are because their focus is solely on what you do. If Judas could have just realized who Jesus really was then, he wouldn't have had so much disdain for what He was doing or not doing.

Judas had shown behaviors of betrayal, but the act of betrayal did not take place like I would have imagined it would. When I hear betrayal I picture Judas rolling into the garden on the back of a tank with a megaphone, yelling, "That's Him, over there! Get Him!" But Judas calmly greeted Jesus and then kissed Him on the cheek. The most infamous betrayal in the history of the world was not executed through a war or a riot, but through a kiss.

There are few things in life more intimate than a kiss. I believe this is an important detail in the narrative because it speaks to the false intimacy that betrayers often convey. They want you to think they're close to you, but their kiss is not one of respect or affection; it is one of contempt and affliction. Their kiss is strategic. It means they're close enough to hurt you. Judas will kiss you on the cheek and stab you in the back simultaneously.

With Friends Like These—Who Needs an Enemy?

It's human nature to want to focus on the actual act of betrayal. It hurts, it's messy, and it often comes from a person or place you never would have imagined.

So far, I believe I've focused too much on the act of betrayal, and not enough on our actions after the betrayal. I know I'm guilty of this. In my life, when I've been betrayed, I want to stop the story right there; close the book, that's it, the end. I want to wallow in the discomfort of the present circumstance. I want to know why the person so close to me betrayed me. I want to know how long they've been planning to stab me in the back. I want to know who helped them, and how much they received for my betrayal. I want to ask them what I did that made them turn from a disciple to a deceiver.

When I've been betrayed in the past, I didn't have many nice things to say to my betrayers. And admittedly, I probably could have handled some of those situations with much more restraint and decency. It was easy to want to get revenge, to lash out, and to try to cause the betrayer as much pain as he or she caused me.

One of the most fascinating details of this betrayal in the garden was that after Judas completed the betrayal by kissing Jesus, Jesus called Judas a name. I have to be honest; it's not the name I would have called the person who just betrayed me. Oh, don't get me wrong; I would have called Judas some names, and then would have had to wash my mouth out with soap, ala *A Christmas Story*. The names I have called my betrayers cannot be published. (Don't judge me. You know you've done it too.)

Jesus calls Judas a name that I would not have chosen. He doesn't call him a betrayer, backstabber, snake, devil, or evil spirit. He doesn't call Judas a deceiver, con artist, rat, turncoat, or two-face. He doesn't even call Judas prideful, jealous, a person with inverted values, selfish, or fake. So what name did Jesus call Judas by just seconds after being betrayed? What name did Jesus call the one He had mentored over the last three years who had stabbed Him in the back? Jesus called him "friend."

> **"Jesus called Judas friend because He could see past the pain of the present, and realized Judas was necessary for the fulfillment of His future."**

How could Jesus call Judas a friend? How could Jesus ever consider someone a friend who had just betrayed Him? I could never have called a backstabber a friend. That's not what a friend does. A friend doesn't think they're better than you. A friend isn't jealous of you. And a friend doesn't sell you for a few pieces of silver when you've treated him like gold. A friend doesn't live his life taking from you—that's not friendship. And a friend definitely doesn't betray you. Yet, despite what Judas had just done, Jesus called him friend.

Jesus called Judas friend because He could see past the pain of the present, and realized Judas was necessary for the fulfillment of His future. Could it be that Judas was exactly what Jesus needed to take the next step toward His destiny? Jesus was showing us that even though betrayals cut deeper than we thought possible, they also might push us further than we could have imagined. Jesus called Judas friend because even though the betrayal hurt, it helped.

Dive Into Five Questions

1. What areas of your life do you filter to make look better than they really are? Why do you feel the need to filter those areas?
2. What is your first instinct when you've been betrayed?
3. What should your first instinct be?
4. How have you treated people who have betrayed you? What have you said about them? What names have you called them?
5. What must you do to get to a place where you can call a betrayer "friend"?

CHAPTER TEN
THANK YOU, JUDAS

A couple of years ago a series of tornados swept across central Oklahoma and produced an extensive path of destruction which grew to 1.3 miles wide and seventeen miles long. The city of Moore, Oklahoma was hit the hardest. Winds reached 300 mph as an EF5 tornado ripped the area apart with no apologies. There were twenty-four deaths and 377 people injured. The overall damage of the twister was estimated at $2 billion.

    I remember watching Fox News and CNN and seeing the story unfold. I saw countless photographs of destroyed buildings, schools, and dreams. People were in complete shock: their homes, places of employment, and way of life were gone. I remember thinking; *I wish we could do something to help.* So we did. Our nonprofit organization, Hope Pushers, organized a thirty-mile run to raise money for the victims of the tornados. We called it, "Running 4 Relief." We raised $5,000 and partnered with area churches to help bring a little bit of hope to what seemed like a hopeless situation. Countless generous individuals, churches, celebrities, and organizations donated funds to help rebuild the area affected by the tornados. We stand with Moore and still pray for them to this day.

On a much smaller scale, tornados of betrayal can rip through our lives at times. Much like a physical tornado, it's not so much the wind, rain, and change in climate that bring the most devastation; it's the path of destruction the tornado leaves behind that causes the most discouragement and despair. In a similar way, an act of betrayal can be terribly painful. But that is just the beginning of the damage, not the conclusion of it. The act of betrayal is hard, but it's the path of destruction betrayal leaves behind that can be most devastating.

Betrayal is terrible, but betrayal by someone close to you hurts even more. And I've learned that the initial betrayal is usually just the start of a long painful process. I wish it weren't that way, but it's true. It's not so much the betrayal that causes the most pain; it's the aftereffects of the betrayal that can make you go crazy.

Jesus stood in the Garden of Gethsemane with the scent of betrayal still on His cheek. Judas, one of His closest friends and followers, had just kissed Him, and by doing so, identified Him as the one to be taken into custody. The kiss in the garden was the genesis of the betrayal. What came next was worse than Judas could have imagined. The events that unfolded were more than a simple betrayal; they unleashed a story that would change the course of history. It was a kiss that changed eternity.

Path to the Cross

After Jesus was kissed, He was arrested and taken into custody by Roman soldiers. He had been betrayed by someone close to Him, and now He would have to endure the shame, pain, and ridicule that would follow. In a moment, He was taken from a place of prayer to the position of a prisoner. The betrayal was shocking, at least to the other disciples, but it was the next part of the story that was the most painful.

Jesus was sent to the whipping post. This was a post to which a prisoner would remain tied while he received his punishment. The soldiers used a kind of whip called a "cat-o'-nine-tails." This ancient torture tool was a made up of nine tails, and shards of glass, bone, and metal were attached to each one. Each time the whip connected with the back of Jesus, the glass, bones and metal dug into His skin. And with every recoil of the punisher's wrist, parts of His flesh were ripped off. What Jesus endured at the whipping post would kill most men. But Jesus wasn't most men. He wasn't even mostly man. He was God, and with each stripe on His back He was buying back our healing. The Bible says, *"But He was wounded for our transgressions, He was bruised for our iniquities; The chastisement for our peace was upon Him, And by His stripes we are healed"* (Isaiah 53:5, NKJV). Our healing was sealed on the back of Jesus. Jesus was stabbed in the back by Judas and beaten on the back at the whipping post so He would have our back and buy back our healing.

The betrayal in the garden led to the arrest of Jesus and to His beating at the whipping post. The pain didn't stop there though; the story continued. His beard was plucked, hair by hair. He was stripped naked of all earthly garments. The only things that covered Him were a greater purpose and the grace of God. A crown made from thorns was pushed down onto His head in an attempt by his torturers to mock the fact that He was the "King of the Jews." The sharp thorns sunk deep into His head as He made His way to Golgotha to be crucified.

The pain was so intense that Jesus could barely carry His own cross. A man named Simon was pulled out of the crowd to carry it for Him. The crowd made its way to the top of Golgotha, the place of the skull. Jesus was thrown on top of the cross and a nail was driven through His feet. Another nail was driven through each of His wrists. The cross was lifted high for all to see. Jesus, a perfect man who had done nothing wrong, died a criminal's death.

It didn't make sense. How could it come to this? A man who had done so much good for so many people was now dying a death reserved for the worst convicts. Judas was so overcome with the emotion of his decision that he went back to the religious leaders, threw the thirty pieces of silver on the floor before them, and departed in hysteria. He knew that his betrayal had led to the death of an innocent man, but He didn't realize that his betrayal led to the fulfillment of God's plan.

God can take our greatest pain and use it for His greater purpose. He can take our betrayals and turn them into blessings. Judas didn't even know what He was doing, but He pushed Jesus towards His destiny. The cross was not what Judas wanted for Jesus, but it's what God wanted. And the instrument of death brought new life. Jesus became the ultimate sacrifice, dying for the sins of the world. Because of His death you and I can have everlasting life.

Shout-out . . .

It's crazy to think that the divine plan and purpose of Jesus coming to planet Earth was set in motion by a betrayal. The fulfillment of numerous prophecies and the miracle of salvation were sparked by Judas's betrayal of Jesus. The way the Bible accounts read (at least the way I read them), it appears Jesus would not have made it to the cross without Judas. Judas didn't hinder Jesus; he helped Him reach His potential. The betrayal was not only part of the plot, but it was necessary for the narrative of Jesus's mission. Judas was essential to Jesus's journey. And every Judas is a paramount part of your journey.

Could it be that every betrayal you've ever gone through helped make you who you are today? I'm not suggesting that you diminish the wounds of the past, but consider that perhaps every pain you've ever endured brought you from where you were to where God wanted you to be. Your betrayers tried to destroy you, but all they accomplished was pushing you towards your destiny.

> "The betrayal was not only part of the plot, but it was necessary for the narrative of Jesus's mission. Judas was essential to Jesus's journey. And every Judas is a paramount part of your journey."

Their backstabbing pushed you into your breakthrough, and their betrayal set you up for a blessing. They kissed you in the garden, killed you at Golgotha, and tried to keep you in the grave. But your decision to not quit and keep going unlocked the next level of greatness inside you. They should have made you bitter, but they made you better. They tried to stop you, but they made you stronger. You have the power to take what happened to you and turn it from a stumbling block into a building block for your future.

Think about it. Every single thing you've ever gone through brought you to the place you are now. Every battle had a purpose, and every struggle had a function. The past pain was a prerequisite for present realities and future promises. Every betrayal was simply a blessing in disguise.

The next time betrayers take action in your life, don't expect an apology. Judas is remorseful, but he is never repentant. The next time you see Judas, don't say, "I hate you," or ask, "How could you?" The next time you see Judas say, "Thank You."

So here's my shout-out to every betrayer, backstabber, deceiver, and traitor. I have nothing but love for you. You were necessary for my development. If you hadn't betrayed me, I might still be where I was when you found me. If you hadn't hurt me, I might still be functioning at only a fraction of my potential. If you hadn't cut me, I might still be operating at a lower level of my calling. I didn't realize it at the time, but every Judas in my life was a catalyst for growth. Judas helped make me who I am today.

> *"The past pain was a prerequisite for present realities and future promises. Every betrayal was simply a blessing in disguise."*

Blessed but Still Broken

You might feel like what you've read in these pages makes sense, but find it's not that easy to thank someone who hurt you so badly. You might agree that in the long run, a betrayal could be beneficial, but right now you still feel broken. Maybe the betrayal was recent. Maybe the wound is still open. Maybe you find yourself in one of the roughest and most difficult seasons of your life. I want you to know that it is possible to be blessed and still be broken.

Thanking Judas does not exonerate him or diminish what you went through. I'm not suggesting that the pain you had to deal with—or are still dealing with—is easy to dismiss. I want you to know it's perfectly okay not to be okay. Thanking Judas is not the completion of the healing process—it's your introduction to it. You might be blessed by something that still has you broken. It is feasible to be blessed and broken concurrently.

This can be seen clearly in one of the most famous sermons ever recorded: the Sermon on the Mount. In this sermon, Jesus encourages His listeners with what we now call the Beatitudes, and says, *"Blessed are the poor in spirit, for theirs is the kingdom of heaven"* (Matthew 5:3, NKJV). In other words, you can be blessed and broken before God. It doesn't have to be either/or. In fact, it's usually both/and.

You might be blessed by betrayal, but you can also be broken by betrayal. You might still be addressing wounds from a friend. You might still be heartbroken over what happened to you. If you are broken, I want you to know you are the perfect candidate for God to use. I've discovered that God only uses broken, imperfect people. Brokenness is a requirement for advancement. The more we are broken, the more we can be used.

Flashback to the Last Supper.

After Judas left the group, Jesus led the other disciples in what we now call Communion. He passed the cup of wine and explained how it was His blood that was shed for them. He also took the bread, blessed it, broke it, and gave it away. He informed the disciples how the bread was His body that was broken for them. Did you catch it?

> "It's the brokenness that unlocks greatness."

The bread was taken, blessed, broken, and then finally given away. You can see this same sequence in the miracle of the feeding of the 5,000 and in the story of the road to Emmaus found in Luke 24. The bread is blessed, but it has to be broken before it can be multiplied.

The more we are broken, the more we can be given away. We can be blessed, but it's the breaking that causes the multiplication. Brokenness doesn't disqualify you. On the contrary, it accelerates your destiny. It's the brokenness that unlocks greatness. You might not have known you had it in you, but Judas pushed it out of you.

Blessed by betrayal, broken by betrayal, but how do you beat betrayal?

Dive Into Five Questions

1. What are some instances when God took your pain and turned it around for your good?
2. Have you ever wanted to quit or give up after being betrayed?
3. What do you have to do to keep yourself from quitting?
4. Recall seasons of your life when you've been broken. Was there purpose on the other side of your pain?
5. What are some steps you can take to move toward healing?

CHAPTER ELEVEN
CATCH AND RELEASE

My parents were out of town and I was in charge of watching my younger sister, Chantyl. Any sixteen-year-old boy knows that watching younger siblings is more like a prison sentence than anything. I was tired of driving her around, fighting over the TV, and arguing over what type of food we should order with the money our parents left for us. We were getting on each other's last nerves. I have no idea what that phrase means, but I think it works in this scenario. So, Chantyl did what any younger sister who was tired of her big brother would do: she planned an attack.

After hogging the TV for hours, I started to walk up the stairs to the second floor where our bedrooms were located. It was late and dark, and eerily quiet. I remember thinking that my sister must have been asleep already, exhausted from the emotional turmoil I had inflicted upon her. I walked up the stairs and through the doorway to my room to be greeted by one of the scariest moments of my life.

Chantyl had been patiently sitting in the dark, for who knows how long, waiting for me to enter my room. As I walked into room she let out the loudest, scariest, creepiest "BOO" in the history of civilization. It scared me half to death, and I let out a scream that would cause some to question my manhood.

She thought she had accomplished her mission. She had frightened her big brother to the brink of a nervous breakdown. She found satisfaction in my sheer terror. But what came next she didn't see coming, literally or metaphorically.

Little did Chantyl know, but I was planning on reading a little bit before going to sleep, and I was carrying a book in my hands. So, after screaming like a baby I did something without thinking about it. I launched the book with all my might toward my late night attacker. I didn't know it was my sister, and my instincts had kicked in. (I'd like to take this moment to once again apologize to Chantyl: I'm sorry.) The euphoria she felt from scaring me was soon replaced by sheer terror at the paperback traveling at top speed toward her face. I think she still has a bruise—at least emotionally. To this day, she has never tried to scare me again. (Smart girl.)

The fact that I connected with a fiction fastball from two feet away was not enough for me. Chantyl went to bed, but I stayed up for hours planning my revenge. I had screamed like a girl at a Justin Bieber concert, and I was humiliated. A book throw did not compensate my pride. What could I do?

The next night, I flipped the script. I conveniently let Chantyl watch the TV, and I "went to bed" (and by "went to bed," I meant "planned my attack"). I changed into all black clothes, went into Chantyl's room, hid in her closet, and waited. My plan was a more spiritual, weird, "there's someone in my closet" attack. So as my sister got into her bed and tried to go to sleep, I began to whisper things like, "I see you," so quietly I could barely hear myself say them. (Super creepy, huh? That was what I was going for.)

I continued this until I heard Chantyl start to pray out loud and plead the blood of Jesus over her life. I felt vindicated. My work there was done. I popped out of her closet for one last scare, turned on the light, and told her she got was she deserved for scaring me the previous night. Oh, the joys of being a big brother. (In case you're wondering, Chantyl and I have a good relationship now, and there is no long-term baggage stemming from these incidents.)

Retribution . . .

From scaring my sister to countless other examples, I've discovered that when I've been wronged, my first instinct is to seek revenge. It's human nature to try to hurt someone and make them feel the same pain they caused you. When someone betrays you, it's easy to try to get back at them.

If I were Jesus, I don't think I could have spent over three years with Judas, knowing what he was going to do. And after Judas betrayed me, I sure wouldn't have called him my friend. I would have tried to convince God to allow the cross to cover for the sins of the whole world, except for Judas. Thank God I'm not Jesus. I would have messed it all up.

What we have to remember is that revenge is not our responsibility. It's not up to us to right what's been wronged. It's not our job to get even. Revenge might cause temporary satisfaction, but it will bring eternal consequences.

Jesus could have sought revenge. He could have made Judas feel the same way He felt. When you've been betrayed, it's natural to plan and devise a strategy for vindication. But Jesus didn't lash out at or condemn Judas. He loved Judas, called him a friend, and then went and died on a cross for him.

The Bible tells us that Judas felt so bad about what he had done that he went out, found a tree, and hung himself. I've discovered that if you just love people who hurt you, Jesus will take care of the vengeance. If you just befriend people who betray you, Judas will usually hang himself. We don't have to worry about getting even. Our responsibility is to love people, not level the playing field.

The Judas in your life will almost always find a way to hurt himself. The trendy terminology is to call this "karma," but the Bible speaks of a principle of sowing and reaping. *"Do not be deceived: God cannot be mocked. A man reaps what he sows"* (Galatians 6:7, NIV). Don't worry about getting revenge. Judas always gets what is coming to him. We should not take pleasure in the pain of Judas, but we should find peace in the fact that retribution is up to God, not left to us.

Forgive and Remember

If we allow our need for revenge to go unchecked, it will create an opportunity to produce unforgiveness. If you're not careful, you'll end up spending more energy getting even than you do getting healed. That's not healthy, and it hurts you more than it hurts Judas.

That's why it is so imperative to catch the seeds of unforgiveness before they take root in your spirit. Unresolved unforgiveness can ruin your life. If you fail to forgive others, the Bible says that God will not forgive you: *"But if you refuse to forgive others, your Father will not forgive your sins"* (Matthew 6:15). It's not that He can't or is unable—He won't.

That verse is one that people often don't like to quote. It doesn't make many people's "life scriptures" list. It's straightforward, and it hits hard. We will be forgiven in proportion to how forgiving we are to others. We need to forgive people who hurt us? Even Judas? Yes, if you want to be forgiven.

Here's where most people get hung up: They think that if they forgive Judas for what he's done to them, they're saying what he did was acceptable. Forgiving someone doesn't excuse or validate what they did. Forgiveness is not a gift you give someone else. It is a gift you give yourself. Lewis B. Smedes said, "To forgive is to set a prisoner free and discover that the prisoner was you."

No matter how much a person hurt you, or how deep the wound was, you have to make a conscience decision to catch yourself before unforgiveness and resentment take over your life. When you forgive someone, you're not agreeing with what they did, you are simply saying that you're not going to allow pain from the past to negatively alter the promises of your future.

> "Forgiveness is not a gift you give someone else. It is a gift you give yourself."

Not only should you have some gratitude for Judas, but you shouldn't hold a grudge against him. So many of us are nursing grudges from past wounds. When you fail to eliminate unforgiveness in your life it stop wounds from becoming scars. Scars are wounds that have been treated and healed. Wounds are fresh, untreated pains that need your attention. Your wounds need treatment, but your scars are your testimony. Don't be ashamed or afraid to talk about your wounds. There's power in sharing what you've overcome. You should mend your wounds, but you should mouth your scars.

The best way to get revenge is to forgive people when they don't "deserve" it. We think holding a grudge gives us the power over the person who hurt us, don't we? The opposite is true. When you fail to forgive someone, you are actually giving them the power over you.

So, no matter the magnitude of their betrayal, no matter how much they hurt you, do yourself a favor and forgive them. The healing process not only includes thanking Judas, but it also includes forgiving Judas. Remember to catch unforgiveness before it turns to resentment, and put a stop to it. Forgiveness will set you free. Are you ready?

How do you forgive someone?
Here are three steps that have helped me:
1. Ask God to help you
2. Pray for them daily
3. Remember that God has forgiven you

I'm not saying that forgiving someone who hurt you will be easy, but it is essential for your continued growth. Choose to forgive them today. Let the restoration process begin. Take back control of your life. You won't move forward until you move past the past.

Re-Lease

I'm not much of a fisherman. I'm not much of an outdoorsman at all, to be honest. My idea of "roughing it" is staying in a three-star hotel. I believe camping should be reserved for punishment, not pleasure. Some people love the camping experience: sleeping in tents, fighting bugs, being chased by wild animals. I can't think of many things worse than that.

I have gone fishing a few times and enjoyed it on most occasions. I am the guy who needs help baiting his hook. (I know you were wondering.)

One time, I went fishing with a family friend on a lake in Minnesota. I can't tell you which one of the 10,000 lakes it was—sorry. My friend caught a fish. It was a big fish—one I thought would be a "keeper," but he threw it back into the water. I asked him why he hadn't kept such a nice fish. He informed me that he was practicing a technique of conservation called "catch and release." All day long we caught fish, but then released them back into the water in order to preserve them.

Not only do you have to thank Judas and forgive Judas, but you also have to release Judas. How do you really know when you've forgiven someone completely, released him or her, and let go of what he or she did to you? True healing begins when you not only thank and forgive your betrayers, but you release them. This is a technique of conservation and preservation of your sanity, health, and soul.

When you release the pain and grudges from your hands, you are giving yourself a new lease on joy, peace, and your future. You are basically "re-leasing" all that God has in store for you. You're establishing a new lease on your life. I've discovered that oftentimes, God's hands and my hands are linked. God won't release the healing in His hands until I release the pain out of my hands. It's powerful when you can not only forgive, but also let go of anything that is holding you back from your future. The best way to get a clear view of your tomorrow is to stop looking in the rearview mirror of your yesterday.

Thank Judas. Forgive Judas. Release Judas
Learn from your pain, don't wallow in it.
Let your wounds turn into scars.
This is how you beat betrayal.

One More Thing . . .

I've discovered that life is a series of adjustments and stretches. I've learned that, unfortunately, there is more than one Judas I'll have to deal with in my lifetime. At times, it can seem that just as I finish thanking one Judas, another one enters the scene. I wish that weren't the case, but it seems to be the way it goes. I wish each person only had to beat betrayal once, but I don't think that's how it works.

There is one more interesting part of the story of Judas. The first chapter of the book of Acts records the disciples casting lots to decide who would take Judas's place. If you had to use a more modern analogy, you could say that Judas was replaced using a coin flip. The position of Judas—the betrayer who hung himself—was decided by the equivalent of "heads or tails." The very thing that Judas received for betraying Jesus was the same thing used to find his replacement—a coin.

What am I saying?

Judas is easily replaceable. I hope you don't have to encounter numerous betrayers in your life, but I want you to know you will most likely face more than one. But this is good news. The bigger the attack, the bigger the calling on your life. With every Judas comes promotion.

It's all a matter of perspective. Don't let people who hurt you steal your joy. Don't let Judas derail you. Don't let pains from your past dictate your future. Your future is so bright.

There is healing on the other side of your hurt. There is purpose behind the pain. Every Judas from your past, present, and future will accomplish one thing: they will push you towards your destiny.

The best is yet to come.

Thank you, Judas.

Dive Into Five Questions

1. What are some instances in your life when you tried to get back at someone?
2. Have you ever tried to "get even"?
3. Did getting even make you feel like you thought it would?
4. Make a list of people you need to forgive. How can you forgive these people and get a new lease on life?
5. How can you turn bitterness into thankfulness for those who've hurt you?

CPSIA information can be obtained
at www.ICGtesting.com
Printed in the USA
FFOW04n1551091016
28254FF